HOW TO
WRITE FOR
UNIVERSITY

HOW TO
WRITE FOR
UNIVERSITY

KATHLEEN McMILLAN
JONATHAN WEYERS

PEARSON

Harlow, England • London • New York • Boston • San Francisco • Toronto • Sydney
Auckland • Singapore • Hong Kong • Tokyo • Seoul • Taipei • New Delhi
Cape Town • São Paulo • Mexico City • Madrid • Amsterdam • Munich • Paris • Milan

Pearson Education Limited
Edinburgh Gate
Harlow CM20 2JE
United Kingdom
Tel: +44 (0)1279 623623
Web: www.pearson.com/uk

First Published 2014 (print and electronic)

ISBN: 978-1-292-00150-0 (print)
      978-1-292-00646-8 (CseTxt)
      978-1-292-00647-5 (PDF)

British Library Cataloguing-in-Publication Data
A catalogue record for the print edition is available from the British Library

Library of Congress Cataloging-in-Publication Data
A catalog record for the print edition is available from the Library of Congress

10 9 8 7 6 5 4 3 2 1
18 17 16 15 14

Print edition typeset in 9.5pt Helvetica Neue by 3
Print edition printed and bound in Great Britain by Ashford Colour Press Ltd, Gosport

NOTE THAT ANY PAGE CROSS REFERENCES REFER TO THE PRINT EDITION

CONTENTS

WRITING TECHNIQUE – HOW TO PLAN AND WRITE FOR ASSESSMENT

DEVELOPING FUTURE ACADEMIC WRITING – HOW TO BUILD ON MARKERS' ADVICE FOR GOOD RESULTS

APPENDICES

PREFACE AND ACKNOWLEDGEMENTS

We are pleased that you have chosen **How to write for university – academic writing for success** and we hope that it will help you with all your academic writing tasks, regardless of your experience and background. Our aim has been to provide a book that follows a straightforward sequence of 12 steps to writing a successful assignment at university. Along the way, we take you through the phases of understanding the university assessment process, gathering information, processing the ideas in preparation for creating writing and integrating your new knowledge and skill into future assignments and exams. We've complemented all of this by adding tips and ideas that we hope will help you build a strong foundation for writing well. At the back of the book you will find appendices to help you with key information and examples of skills such as creating notes, framing outline plans and using referencing styles, as well as technical aspects of punctuation, spelling and grammar. We've tried to remain faithful to the philosophy of our other books in the *Smarter Student* series by creating an accessible resource that can guide you in completing your university assignments and act as a reference that you can dip into as your studies progress. We hope that it will meet your needs.

We would like to offer sincere thanks to many people who have influenced us and contributed to the development and production of this book. Countless students over the years have helped us to test our ideas, especially those whose written work we have commented on, supervised and assessed. We are grateful to the following colleagues and collaborators who have helped us directly or indirectly: Margaret Adamson, Michael Allardice, John Berridge, Richard Cambell, Steven Duncan, Margaret Forrest, Neil Glen, Anne-Marie Greenhill, Jane Illés, Bill Kirton, Eric Monaghan, Fiona O'Donnell, Richard Parsons, Jane Prior, Mhairi Robb, Anne Scott, Dorothy Smith, Gordon Spark, David Walker, Amanda Whitehead and David Wishart.

Also, we acknowledge those at other universities who have helped frame our thoughts, particularly our good friends, Rob Reed, Nicki Hedge and Esther Daborn. We owe a special debt to the senior colleagues who encouraged various projects that contributed to this book, and who allowed us freedom to pursue this avenue of scholarship, especially Robin Adamson, Chris Carter, Ian Francis, Rod Herbert and David Swinfen. At Pearson Education, we have had excellent advice from Steve Temblett, Rob Cottee, Lucy Carter and Priyadharshini Dhanagopal. Finally, we would like to say thanks to our long-suffering but nevertheless enthusiastic families: Derek, Keith, Nolwenn, Fiona, Tom and Eilidh; and Mary, Paul and James, all of whom helped in various capacities.

ABOUT THE AUTHORS

Dr Kathleen McMillan was formerly Academic Skills Advisor and Senior Lecturer, University of Dundee.

Dr Jonathan Weyers was formerly Director of Quality Assurance, University of Dundee.

Both are now freelance authors specialising in books on skills development in Higher Education.

This book represents a synthesis based on over 60 years of combined advisory, teaching and administrative experience, at undergraduate and postgraduate levels. Our backgrounds in the Arts and Humanities and Life Sciences respectively mean that our support has covered a wide range of subjects – from biology to orthopaedic surgery, information and communication technology to law, as well as English as a foreign language.

Above all, we have spoken to countless students, both individually and in focus groups, and have consulted with fellow academics about the skills that underpin a wide range of disciplines.

We have carried out a number of relevant projects, most notably the writing and editing of an extensive Website providing guidance for undergraduates and postgraduates studying at the University of Dundee. Our collaborative writing has resulted in eight books on diverse aspects of learning and writing at university level. Most of these have appeared in several editions and they have been translated into a total of seven other languages.

In short, we have read widely, thought deeply about relevant issues and tested many ideas related to the undergraduate learning and postgraduate research writing. This book is a distillation of all the best tips and techniques we've come across or have developed ourselves.

INTRODUCTION

1

THE IMPORTANCE OF WRITING AT UNIVERSITY

How your abilities in academic writing contribute to your success

Writing is a challenging and fulfilling activity. For students, it brings together all their relevant knowledge and understanding of a topic in response to a particular task – but it is more than that. From completing your writing tasks, you will gain skills in the use of language and effective communication. In addition, you will carry the associated critical thinking skills with you into your professional life after university. This chapter explains the importance of writing for academic purposes at university – both now and in the future.

KEY TOPICS

→ Writing and the process of communication

→ How this book is organised

KEY UNIVERSITY TERMS

Critical thinking   Professional body

Writing is a skill that will not be confined to your university days. Indeed, your ability to use the transferable skill of writing will mark you as a competent communicator of facts and opinions. In your professional life, in all sorts of contexts and for all sorts of purposes you will draw on the training you receive at university in presenting your ideas effectively on paper. However, it takes time and dedication to acquire and develop the competence in writing that you will need. This book is about how you can develop your skill in academic writing from the very start of your university studies so that it becomes an effective tool of communication within your skill set.

What is academic writing?

Universities have been around for a long time and have evolved over the years in many respects. However, one feature that remains constant is the need to present work for assessment in writing. While the technology that makes printed or electronic submission possible is relatively new, little has changed about the fundamental features that characterise acceptable academic writing – even when word-processed.

Thus, academic writing is an expression of logic that is the product of thinking. This means that the writing that you produce is a reflection of your intellectual abilities. It puts into words your knowledge and your conceptual understanding, and shows evidence of your ability to think critically. Furthermore, it demonstrates your competence in expressing higher-order concepts by, for example, expressing opinions based on thorough analysis, synthesis and evaluation of multiple sources. Thus, academic writing has to be planned, concise and relevant to the task set and the nature of the form of writing you have been asked to produce. By observing these characteristics, you will gain good marks for your work.

WRITING AND THE PROCESS OF COMMUNICATION

Writing is a vehicle for communicating thought to others. Your ability to do this effectively is important because:

- it shows that you can meet the expectations and marking criteria for those who grade your work (**Ch 2**, **Ch 8** and **Ch 13**)

- it demonstrates your intellectual abilities to others (**Chs 2–13**)

- it identifies you as a higher-order thinker who can engage with more sophisticated ideas and integrate the essence of that thinking into your own work (**Ch 8**, **Ch 9**, **Ch 11** and **Ch 12**)

- it demonstrates your ability to analyse and explain complex ideas to others (**Ch 11**, **Ch 12** and **Ch 14**)

- it provides evidence of your problem-solving abilities based on sound argument and counter-argument (**Chs 9–11**)

- it illustrates your competence as an effective communicator to future employers (**Chs 14–17**)

- it shows that you are able to apply and adapt new learning from one area to meet the requirements of other contexts (**Chs 17–19**).

From this overview, it can be seen that developing your skill in academic writing is a challenging process and one that you need to develop over time. It requires commitment and patience to learn how to develop your writing through the drafting, crafting and re-drafting that are part of the evolutionary passage of every assignment from rough notes to final version. Learning how to write to the high standard expected at university will be a longer-term investment for your career.

HOW THIS BOOK IS ORGANISED

By dividing the book into four sections, we provide coverage that will allow you to understand and develop skills that may be particular to a specific stage in the writing process and that, taken together, will help you to produce high-quality written work that 'ticks all the boxes' both intellectually and in presentational terms.

1 **Essentials for getting started** – how to gather and record information. These chapters begin the in-depth scrutiny of how academic writing comes about through the gathering of information that forms the basis of your understanding and comes from a variety of sources (**Chs 2–7**).

2 **Understanding the contexts and practices relating to academic writing** – how to meet the standards expected of you in order to achieve good marks. These chapters provide essential insights into what you have to do to prepare your writing for assessment (**Chs 8–13**).

3 **Writing technique** – how to plan and write for assessment. These chapters explain the practical steps you need to follow to use the information you have gathered and processed to support the writing your produce (**Chs 14–17**).

4 **Developing future academic writing** – how to build on writing advice for good results in exams and later writing. The final chapters suggest ways in which you can develop your writing further by capitalising on feedback and your own experience (**Chs 18–19**).

Therefore, this book is about helping you to achieve good writing by adopting a 12-step approach that takes you through information gathering and processing, creating writing to university standard and developing your writing for future assignments including exams. Table 1.1 shows the twelve steps to achieving this and how they relate to the chapters in this book.

Table 1.1 A subdivision of a large writing task into 12 manageable steps

Subdivision	Typical actions	Chapter
Step 1 Consult course or module handbook	• verify assignment dates • consider nature and wording of assignment • note learning outcomes for the assignment	2, 13
Step 2 Identify relevant/recommended material	• create lecture/tutorial/lab notes • consult reading list and any in-lecture references	2–7
Step 3 Research/obtain material	• access source material via on-site library or online	4
Step 4 Read material	• frame notes for relevance to assignment	5, 6
Step 5 Analyse wording of assignment	• identify what you are being instructed to do	8, 9
Step 6 Reflect on the topic	• evaluate the response that you will construct	8–12
Step 7 Plan your writing	• ensure good fit with standard framework	15-17
Step 8 Create a first draft	• shape your academic writing style; use critical thinking and avoid plagiarism	16
Step 9 Finalise reference list	• construct the list of supporting materials as you write	12, 16, 17
Step 10 Review text for submission	• edit and proof-read	13, 16, 17
Step 11 Consider feedback	• assess how to modify content and technique for inclusion in your future written assignments	18
Step 12 Modify academic writing for exam conditions	• use feedback to contribute to revision and to adjust writing for exam purposes	19

PRACTICAL TIPS FOR UNDERSTANDING THE IMPORTANCE OF WRITING

Adjusting your thought processes and perspectives. The essential adjustment that most people need to make, especially in the early stages of being a university student, is to their mind-set. This may mean taking conscious steps to become more questioning about what you hear and read so that you become a more independent thinker. It may also require you to accept that you need to develop a wider competency in skills that may have been introduced to you at school or college; these will need to be upgraded for university learning, thinking and writing.

Learn more about the writing styles used in your subject area. Writing a 'tweet' or a holiday postcard is informal communication with restrictions dictated by the medium or the area of paper available. However, writing for academic purposes requires a more formal approach based on more space and fewer linguistic restrictions. Scrutinise your own writing to see how you use the language and structures that are well suited to the more formal style and vocabulary expected at university.

Learn more about how you are expected to write for professional life. Many of the tasks you will be asked to undertake at university are designed to prepare you for writing in your professional life. Once you graduate you will probably need to adapt your writing skills further in order to meet the 'house style' of your employer or, perhaps, the style expected of your professional body. Seeking out and surveying some such professional material – for example, in-house journals, reports or printed publicity – will help to give you an understanding of what you might be expected to produce.

GO And now ...

1.1 Review the skills you bring with you to university. University will be new to you and to your peers. If university learning were not something very special, then there would be no point in becoming a student. Think at the outset about your strengths and weaknesses in the academic context. You may have to take a candid look at aspects that might not be as strong as required for study at this level. Some skills you will have but perhaps not at the level required for university, other skills you may not have at all – and writing for university purposes may fall into this category. Look back at the contents page of this book and consider the overview of what academic writing requires so that you can appreciate the wider implications of developing writing at this level.

1.2 Audit your mind-set. As part of the process of adjusting your mind-set to the new analytical contexts of studying at university, think about what currently influences your thinking. For example, you may read newspapers or websites that promote a particular position or viewpoint. This could be based on political, pressure group or cultural standpoints and such content can shape the ideas of their readership. Appraise the sources that influence your own thinking and assess whether the views you develop are based on sound reasoning and verified evidence rather than hearsay, bias, unsupported opinion or sensationalism.

1.3 Think about your writing skills in the context of employment. Look at job advertisements in professional journals, in national newspapers or online. Note how often posts advertised require applicants with 'good communication skills'. This includes the skill of writing so you should consider just how confidently you could state that your writing skills might meet these requirements and how you might provide evidence of this – one obvious place would be in the letter you write to accompany your c.v. and another would be in the c.v. itself. Many an application has come to grief at the beginning of the selection process because of grammatical or spelling errors in the application documents.

ESSENTIALS FOR GETTING STARTED – HOW TO GATHER AND RECORD RELEVANT INFORMATION

2

UNIVERSITY WRITING IN CONTEXT

How your academic writing is shaped from the very start of your course

Writing is an essential skill for university. It shapes your thinking and learning. When you write for university, you show your understanding of your subject and your ability to think clearly and analytically about it. This chapter introduces what you need to know to succeed as an academic writer at university.

KEY TOPICS

→ Making sense of your university context

→ Writing for assessment

→ The inputs to learning and writing

→ The academic skills you'll need for university

→ How inputs and outputs are linked for learning at university

KEY UNIVERSITY TERMS

Curriculum   Module   Note-making   Note-taking   Semester

Whatever your course, understanding the learning environment in which you will study is the foundation of developing your academic writing. You need to identify and interpret the practices and conventions that are particular to university study so that you meet the writing standards expected of you. This means absorbing practical details such as:

● outlines of course content

● how your course will be taught

● how you will be assessed and

● what you will be expected to have accomplished at a number of staging points over the academic year.

This chapter will help you to sort out the detail of the information so that it begins to make sense to you as you become more involved in your course and the writing you need to do.

MAKING SENSE OF YOUR UNIVERSITY CONTEXT

It would not be unusual in these early days if you find that your head is full of snippets of information about these practical matters, and entwined in the mix will be expressions that may or may not be meaningful to you at this stage. Some of this information may be explained in course handbooks (**Step 1**), but some of it you'll just be expected to understand. Figure 2.1 shows some of the more common terms you'll meet and reflects the random way in which they are accumulated. Table 2.1 gives a brief explanation of how universities work so that you understand some of the terms used and functions that people perform to support your learning. These systems and people will play key roles in assessing your performance, especially your writing.

Figure 2.1 Words from early introduction to your course. Some of these words may be meaningful to you, others less clear. You can find definitions in the glossary at the end of this book.

✔ Learning your way about and discovering the specific facilities available to support your learning will be an early priority. Often there are campus tours to help you orientate yourself – sometimes provided centrally or by senior students. Taking time to do this will help you find your feet and often contact with an 'insider' who can answer questions that may not have occurred to you before you arrived.

University is a distinctive learning experience and most students find within their first few months of study at this level that they have to adjust their ways of studying and learning. They need to engage with new content, new material, new ways of teaching and, by implication, new ways of processing information.

As a student, you are expected to take responsibility for your own learning – that means that you are expected to be or become an independent learner early in your studies. Therefore, you'll have to begin sorting out the apparently random and unconnected ideas and terms shown in Figure 2.1. This chapter will 'unpack' some of these terms as they are used in the academic world (Table 2.1) and demonstrate how you can make sense of what will be expected of you – regardless of your course, your discipline or your previous learning.

What you need to know about the practical aspects of assessment

■ Assessment involves different outputs for different disciplines and you may have to produce work in all or some of the types listed in this chapter.

■ The general pattern is that you have to submit coursework to a deadline. Penalties may be imposed if your submission is late. The policy that applies to you will be found in the course handbook.

■ This coursework may involve a range of different types of assignments that are designed to ensure that you fulfil certain outcomes (sometimes called 'learning objectives'), for example, being able to explain a process, identify a cause and effect relationship, analyse a dataset, solve problems or perform an experiment. Such learning outcomes (or objectives) should be listed in the course guide or handbook.

■ Your work will be assessed and graded against a standard scale stipulated in university regulations in relation to the relevant learning outcomes.

■ Although a number of subjects include modes of assessment that do not involve long-form essay-type writing, most require an element of technical writing at some stage in the curriculum. The principles that apply to extensive academic writing (the focus in this book) also apply in technical writing.

Table 2.1 Understanding the university system – knowing how the system operates and how it deals with your assignments will aid your writing.

The place
Your university campus may be urban or rurally based, but the area occupied by the university buildings can be seen as a 'city within a city'. Each university has its own customs and rhythms. Its own specialist personnel often replicate mainstream services exclusively for students. These might include a medical centre, chaplaincy, banks, bookshops, cafés, bars, general or specialist libraries, internet access and sports facilities.

The people
Students and staff form the academic community. Students come from diverse backgrounds to study diverse subjects. University staff are the constant – and the lecturing, researching and administrative staff all make a contribution to providing the education and research opportunities that set universities apart from colleges and schools.
Advisors of Studies (AOS), sometimes called **Directors of Studies (DOS)**, are the lecturers from your department or school who meet you in the first instance to confirm your course choice and prepare your papers for enrolment, sometimes called registration or matriculation.
Lecturers. You'll find that your lecturers are possibly less high-profile than teaching staff in colleges or schools. This is because they have multiple roles to fulfil – in teaching, researching and contributing to the administration of courses. Therefore, you'll usually only encounter lecturers in the formal lecture context and sometimes in the less formal laboratory sessions or tutorials. They are the people who set assessments and exam papers. Senior teaching staff often fulfil the roles of **Course Directors** for particular courses or the teaching programme for a year group. At other times, they will be working on research or administrative matters. If you have problems with written coursework, these are the people you need to approach for guidance.
Tutorial assistants and laboratory demonstrators. These people are often, but not always, postgraduate students, who run specific learning activities – tutorials (in Arts-type subjects) and 'labs' (in Science, Engineering and some Social Science subjects). In addition, they may have responsibility for grading performance in the tutorial/lab and for grading and marking written assignments under the supervision of course directors.
Student support specialists. Support services exist because it is recognised that students may need additional assistance at some points in their university experience. On campus, you will find a range of services including career advice, health care, counselling and study support often including guidance on wider learning issues, but specifically academic writing.

The timetable

Your timetable may not be finalised until your course begins, and often a printed copy of the timetable will not be available until you attend the first lecture when the format will be explained to you. There are distinctions across the disciplines. For example, courses in the Sciences tend to have lectures that, along with tutorials or lab sessions, fill the working day. By contrast, Arts-type courses may have fewer timetabled lectures and tutorials. Typical timetable elements are:

Lectures – usually 50 minutes long with teaching provided by a single lecturer or a series of lecturers who teach in particular weeks over the term or semester.

Tutorials/labs/workshops – students are allocated to particular groups that meet on a regular basis over the period of study. Activities vary from problem-solving, debate of specified issues or prescribed experiments. Your attendance and performance may be part of the course assessment.

Virtual learning environment (VLE) – closed electronic environment that is used in some courses more than others. VLE modules may be used for each module you are taking and will provide you with course information. These will also require your input to prescribed activities such as discussion group or blog contributions. You will need to allocate time for participation since this may form part of the course assessment.

The studying and learning workload

Whatever your subject you will be expected to use your 'free time' on independent study and in preparing written coursework. You will be expected to do this without direction in the more independent learning environment of university, which means that you need to take responsibility for organising yourself and your study time around your timetable of lectures, tutorials and labs and the submission dates for your assessed writing assignments.

Curriculum and assessment. Each university has its own methods of assessment related to its own curriculum (programme of study). Exams and other methods of assessment are particular to that university. Within the UK, for example, standards are monitored by departments, by external examiners, and also by Quality Assurance Agencies.

WRITING FOR ASSESSMENT

To earn your degree, you need to perform as well as you can in assessment. For many students, this need to do well at the highest level can become an end in itself that overshadows the broader aspects of developing knowledge and understanding. Such students often adopt strategic ways of performing so that they can optimise marks by investing more time in some activities than others, for example. This approach only goes so far. It over-simplifies what university learning is all about – the wider profile of skills, intellectual ability, clear thinking and an unbiased approach to new learning are more profound than calculated strategic approaches.

The fact remains that assessment is important and, in the majority of instances, this means writing well to showcase your learning in the best possible way. Look again at Figure 2.1. Some of the words are printed in capital letters. These examples relate to some of the different formats of writing – the output – that you will be expected to produce for assessment. At first glance it might seem that different formats require different skills. Of the six writing episodes listed here, all require a level of literacy and competent writing. However, they differ slightly in approach:

- **Essay** – writing is flexible in terms of structure and content
- **Report** – writing requires a stylised format following subject conventions
- **Blog** – writing spontaneous real-time discussion produced as typed input
- **Quiz** – writing based on one-word or short answers to confirm knowledge
- **Test** – writing for assessment provides responses to monitor understanding
- **Exam** – writing requires time-limited answers and may be either 'short' or essay-type in format.

Your ability to perform in the relevant formats as these apply to your modules will develop as your course progresses. You can read more about assessment in **Ch 14.**

THE INPUTS TO UNIVERSITY LEARNING AND WRITING

The requirement to produce written output suggests that there must be preliminary inputs. Some inputs will be longer term and may in fact pre-date your arrival at university. These might include:

● your familiarity and interest in the subject matter
● your previous learning history and associated writing
● your understanding of what is expected at this level of study.

Since people arrive at university with a collection of different abilities, skills and knowledge, there is some diversity in learning experiences. This mixture of learning backgrounds contributes to the richness of the university experience for all. However, for you as an individual, your learning outputs, especially in writing, will depend on how you respond to the different inputs you are provided within the university system.

Look again at the haphazard collection of words in Figure 2.1. Put aside those words in capital letters (the 'output' words) and then you will see that the remaining lower case words can be loosely termed as 'inputs'. Table 2.2 groups:

● the types of input information sourced through different media
● the particular academic skills that apply to these media
● the types of information that may be offered through these media.

Learning how everything connects is essential to performing well in writing and the associated assessment. Thus, these inputs are preliminaries to learning; how you engage with them will influence your writing significantly.

THE ACADEMIC SKILLS YOU'LL NEED FOR UNIVERSITY

University, for many people, is a unique learning experience and often at the outset many new students are not really aware of the need to 'learn how to learn' at this advanced level. This understanding underpins subject learning on their specific courses. However, often the university system may seem to work from the assumption that students

Table 2.2 Teaching and learning at university. Some inputs come directly through formal or informal teaching activities (lighter shades) while other inputs depend on individual independent study activity (darkest shade).

Source of inputs	Academic skills required	Types of information
• Lectures	• Listening and note-taking	
• Labs • Tutorials • Seminar	• Speaking and practical skills • Listening and speaking • Listening and note-taking	Concepts Evidence Facts

• Library
  – Online sources
  – Specialist journals
• Textbooks
• Handouts/lecture notes provided by staff
• Virtual Learning Environment (VLE) course-specific material
	• Researching, reading and note-making
	• Researching, reading and note-making
	• Reading and note-making
	• Researching, reading and note-making
		Hypotheses
		Ideas
		Knowledge
		Paradigm
		Theory

enter university with these skill sets in place and at the right level for university. This is often not the case and so can mean that students are disadvantaged from the outset unless they firstly recognise that the skill sets are required and, secondly, set about acquiring them.

The following academic skills are typically required in most forms of university study. Each skill will contribute to the development of your academic writing and together they contribute to **Step 2** in the 12-step process leading to academic writing success:

- **Listening skills** – these represent the first challenge new students encounter in lectures, although these skills are required in other academic contexts also. Learning how to listen, understand and learn from what you hear in lectures, tutorials and seminars contributes to the development of your writing (**Ch 3** and **Ch 6**).

- **Researching skills** – these relate to information literacy, especially in gathering information through library facilities. As a new student, going on a library tour is essential in developing these skills and understanding how you can make the most of your library's facilities. Your ability to find the relevant material efficiently will influence the content of your work and the quality of your written presentation of issues or evidence (**Ch 4**).

- **Reading skills** – these relate to learning how the literature in the form of academic texts is structured. This will help you to read more efficiently and quickly. In addition, understanding text structure will influence your own writing (**Ch 5**).

- **Note-taking and note-making skills** – the creation of notes is a skill that will need to be developed in lectures and when reading. You can use your knowledge and understanding of the format of lectures and construction of printed text to create notes that aid your learning. These writing skills are covered in **Ch 6**.

- **Speaking skills** – for academic contexts, these are essential in helping you to formulate ideas and express them orally in discussion or presentation contexts. Such opportunities help you to 'rehearse' the language of a topic and so contribute significantly to structuring academic writing (**Ch 7**).

HOW INPUTS AND OUTPUTS ARE LINKED FOR LEARNING AT UNIVERSITY

In many instances, any output or product is only as good as the input material from which it is derived – in this instance, the input stage is when information is being gathered and the output stage is when the writing related to the information takes place. Between the two, there is a crucial step in understanding, namely, being aware of the contexts and practices – some unspoken – that relate to writing in higher education. A clearer understanding of what these involve will enable you to write well and achieve good marks. This will be considered in greater depth in the second section of this book.

PRACTICAL TIPS FOR UNDERSTANDING THE CONTEXT OF UNIVERSITY WRITING

Check the nature of input material. Study the documents that relate to your course. This is **Step 1** (**Ch 1**) in the 12-step process to success in academic writing as these materials lay out the ground rules that you need to follow to achieve good writing and therefore good marks. Sometimes course or module handbooks are distributed to students in hard copy in the first lectures, or these are presented electronically through the departmental website or virtual learning environment.

Your course handbook will cover all the administration details for the course – term/semester, submission and exam dates and staff details, for example. Depending on the course, the handbook may include information relating to the different modules you will be following or there may be separate handbooks for each module. These documents will normally contain details of course assignments, assessment criteria and reading lists relating to the prescribed tasks. General guidance on how to tackle and present coursework may also be included.

Check out academic language used to explain your course. People who work in large organisations often forget that many of the people they encounter may not be aware of the in-house jargon. University is no exception. Look at the printed material you have been given about your course to see how often some of the words shown in Figure 2.1 have been used in your course/module handbook or in introductory lectures. If you are still unsure what some of these words mean, then look at the glossary in this book.

 **And now ...**

2.1 Get yourself organised. If you have not done so already, obtain an academic diary such as *The Smarter Student Planner*[1], that is, a planner/diary that begins in August and runs across the academic year until the following July. While some people choose to keep an electronic diary, there are advantages in keeping a hard-copy version – it will work even when you have no access to a computer, it gives you an overview of future work and it is easy to update and consult. Furthermore, writing things down can aid memory. Using the diary allows you to plot out the academic year with assignment submission dates, make notes about other course/module activity and to cross-reference these with other module commitments.

2.2 Check for advice on coursework. Your handbook will probably provide guidance on presentation, length and style required for coursework, and you should mark this up for future reference when working on coursework. In addition, teaching staff frequently provide more information in lectures about specific assignments and thus attending all your lectures is important; otherwise, you might miss this particular input.

2.3 Audit your academic writing skills. Consider what writing skills you bring to academic writing. Everyone sometimes makes some mistakes in writing – perhaps because of writing at speed or uncertainty about a particular grammar, spelling or punctuation rule. Go to the **Appendix** section in this book and refresh your memory about particular skills where you might be a little 'rusty' – for example, punctuation, spelling or grammar.

[1] The *Smarter Student Planner* is published annually by Pearson Education and includes material written by the authors of this text.

3

LECTURES, LISTENING AND ACADEMIC WRITING

How information you hear in lectures contributes to your writing

Listening is a key skill – especially in the context of university lectures. The aural information that you receive in lectures and other 'delivery' sessions can make a considerable contribution to your grasp of subject content. Learning how to absorb this information and using it as the groundwork for your research is essential for your understanding and later writing. This chapter provides insights into 'interpreting' what you hear and what you may also decide to record in writing.

KEY TOPICS

→ Why listening in formal lecture contexts is important to writing

→ How lectures are structured

→ Listening and objectivity

→ Gaining information from other listening opportunities

KEY UNIVERSITY TERMS

Aural   Comprehension   Idiomatic   Objectivity   References   VLE

People pick up information in many ways and contexts over a normal day. For students, these range from formal to informal situations (Table 2.2). At the formal end of the spectrum are lectures, academic presentations and debates. Less formal situations include tutorials, seminars, practicals and labs, fieldwork and conversation. In each of these situations, you will find opportunities to gather subject-specific information and so embark on **Step 2** of the 12-step process of writing outlined in **Chapter 1**.

Whatever the situation, you need to separate the relevant and important from what is not academically rigorous (for example, statements founded on diversionary anecdote or subjective opinion rather than strong evidence). Your ability to discriminate between sound and unsound information will develop over time, alongside your skill in creating notes (**Ch 6**).

Practicalities of lectures

Lectures may take different formats according to discipline but some common features are that:

- they are 50 minutes long
- each lecture is slotted into the general course teaching plan
- usually there is no opportunity to ask questions
- time constraints mean that there is little opportunity for repetition of content
- usually no space within the lecture programme to compensate for over-run since different lecturers may contribute to the lecture series on a course or module
- some lecturers may provide handouts pre-lecture for annotation in the lecture or post-lecture to allow for cross comparison with students' own notes; sometimes the 'notes' may be from PowerPoint slides used in the lecture. Note that PowerPoint slides are no substitute for attending the lectures yourself.

WHY LISTENING IN FORMAL LECTURE CONTEXTS IS IMPORTANT TO YOUR WRITING

Lecturers begin preparing their lectures as written text and these lectures are delivered on the basis of printed notes or a scripted text. Hence, the lecture provides:

- presentation of the language and specialist terminologies in the field being examined
- demonstration of how academics think and reason, thus indicating what they expect of you in your writing
- outline coverage of a topic, directing students towards further study from the literature (recommended reading)
- linkage to other lectures or modes of study (for example, tutorial or practical topics) in the series

- a review of different approaches or perspectives on a topic based on evidence, logic, data or other understanding; they may not necessarily provide 'right' or 'wrong' answers to points at issue.

Therefore, students need to:

- analyse the structuring of lecture content as models of thinking and reasoning in their subject area and hence their own writing
- be aware that they will be expected to do follow-up reading to obtain more detailed information and analysis on a topic.

HOW LECTURES ARE STRUCTURED

The format of a lecture is very similar to the format of a good piece of academic writing – an introduction, a main body and a conclusion summarising the key points. Table 3.1 shows the different phases of a lecture and some examples of the corresponding structure of the lecture and modes of explanation of material. These elements are often reflected in the formats of academic writing.

Table 3.1 **Lectures as models of academic format for discussion.** Each subject, lecturer and content will influence the format of a lecture. Becoming aware of lecture structures will guide you in structuring your own writing.

Phases in a lecture	Typical lecture content	Modes of explanation
1. **Introduction** • Aim of lecture • Approach to topic • Identification of key issues 2. **Main body** • Logical analysis of topic or theme 3. **Conclusion** • Review of key points covered in lecture 4. **References** • Information on follow-up reading	• Providing fundamental facts • Analysing and critiquing existing literature • Exploring hypotheses • Examining concepts/theory • Interpreting data or other evidence • Presenting a viewpoint • Refuting a viewpoint • Presenting counter-argument • Problem-solving	• Defining • Categorising/classifying • Describing – Appearance – Location – Structure – Purpose – Use • Giving examples • Cause/effect relationships • Comparing • Contrasting • Listing • Paraphrasing/summarising • Giving entire overview of content

LISTENING AND OBJECTIVITY

Your ability to analyse issues and weigh up evidence both for and against particular positions is key to your university training. Moreover, you are expected to be receptive to new information or new perspectives. Therefore, you need to come to the lecture, seminar or debate with an open mind and a readiness to change your position based on the evidence provided. The balance that you hear presented to you by academics reflects the balance that you will need to achieve in your own oral and written contributions.

GAINING INFORMATION FROM OTHER LISTENING OPPORTUNITIES

The formality of the lecture theatre dictates particular norms in terms of time and style of speaking. However, other listening contexts – the tutorial, the seminar, the debate, even informal classroom chat – offer further opportunities to learn about structuring ideas and explanations. The language will normally be less formal and may even be idiomatic. Nevertheless, the informality of discussion can open opportunities for interruption for counter-argument and insertion of additional points. There is also the opportunity to gauge the groundswell of support on some issues, simply by interpreting body language. These opportunities can help you to evaluate issues and so influence the way that you structure your own discussion on writing. Perceptive students will recognise that idiomatic language is not appropriate for written forms of assessment.

PRACTICAL TIPS FOR LECTURES, LISTENING AND WRITING

What to do if you miss the lecture. The essential advice is 'Don't miss the lecture!', but the reality is that events can overtake the best of intentions and your absence may have been unavoidable. Therefore, should you be unable to attend the lecture for a very good reason, consult the appropriate module on the virtual learning environment to check for lecture notes that may have been posted there by the lecturer. Alternatively, ask a colleague for sight of their notes (however, if you are habitually absent, people may be less keen to lend their notes). Furthermore, there is no guarantee that borrowed notes will be as comprehensive as those you would have taken yourself.

What to do if you can't hear the lecturer or see the visual aids. Speak with or email the lecturer and explain that you found it difficult to hear – giving the reason, if possible. For example, if the air conditioning system affects your ability to hear, then it is possible something may be done about this. If the lecturer does not have a particularly clear voice, you could request that they use a body or lectern microphone. You could sit nearer the front of the lecture theatre to avoid background noise of others speaking, coughing and shuffling of feet.

What to do if you have a seen or unseen disability. Consult with the disability support service in your institution and identify ways in which some assistance might be offered to you, for example, in the provision of a printed handout or PowerPoint slides.

(GO) And now ...

3.1 Map a lecture. Resolve to pay attention to the 'signposts' that lecturers provide in their lecture. These will include reference to aims of the lecture, moving from one point to another, flagging up important points by changes in voice pitch or writing key points on the board or screen, recapping or summarising, especially at the end of a lecture. This will help you understand the structure of the lecture and provide you with understanding of how to present ideas in a logical fashion.

3.2 Listen actively for enriched detail. Sometimes it is useful just to sit back and listen intently to what the lecturer is saying so that you can concentrate on the full thrust of an argument or issue that is being presented to you. To do this, come to an arrangement with a fellow student where you take turns to take notes that you discuss later embellishing them with points that the 'listener' picked up but the 'scribe' did not. In this way you have a set of notes to share that will be more detailed than if you had taken notes independently.

3.3 Listen for new language. A lecture may be the first time that you hear the pronunciation of specialist terms and so this will help you use the same terms correctly. Often new terms are explained in the lecture, but if this is not the case, then you

---

need to note these words down and look them up in a standard dictionary, specialist dictionary or glossary at the end of one of the recommended textbooks on your reading list.

4

RESEARCHING INFORMATION FOR WRITING ASSIGNMENTS

How to use the library as a source of academic information

When writing for academic purposes, you will be expected not only to seek out the books on your reading list but also to source additional material for yourself. This chapter offers some suggestions and strategies for using your library effectively.

KEY TOPICS

→ What do you know already about the reading you need to do?

→ Types of sources that might be recommended to you

→ How to find the resources you need

KEY UNIVERSITY TERMS

Journal   Lateral thinking   Periodical   Procrastination   Synonym

Learning about your university library and how to access its resources is a priority. The library is a key resource for any student. A modern university library is much more than a collection of books and journals – it co-ordinates an electronic gateway to a vast amount of online information not necessarily accessible in other ways. Accessing these resources requires information literacy skills that mean that you can research resources for appropriate and relevant materials. This is **Step 3** in the 12-step process essential for all forms of academic writing.

WHAT DO YOU KNOW ALREADY ABOUT THE READING YOU NEED TO DO?

A library orientation tour or conversation with staff at the help desk will provide you with information about how things are organised in your library. This might include:

- the location of the resources particular to your discipline or course
- the name of the librarian with specific responsibility for helping students in your discipline or on your course
- how to use the electronic catalogue
- how to find a book or periodical
- how you can access the electronic information available to you through your VLE module or library website
- the way to obtain any passwords, if required, to access online resources – depending on the system used. (For example, ATHENS or Shibboleth systems allow publishers to verify that your library has subscribed to an e-resource and that you will have access rights. In some instances access to online resources may be possible without a password through your university's virtual learning environment.)
- how to operate any self-service system of withdrawing books
- how to renew your loan of resources
- how you may be affected by the regulations and codes of conduct, for example, regarding the observation of copyright legislation

Facilities and resources offered by most university libraries

Typically, these may include:

- quiet study areas
- groupwork areas for discussion meetings
- photocopiers and printers
- computing terminals and wifi access
- online catalogue access
- support from expert staff, both in person and via the library website

Apart from books, most UK university libraries will also hold the following in hard copy or with free online access:

- selected daily and weekly newspapers
- periodicals and academic journals
- reference materials
- slides (e.g. for art or life sciences)
- video and DVD resources

TYPES OF SOURCES THAT MIGHT BE RECOMMENDED TO YOU

From your course handbook and lecture information, you will probably have access to a formal reading list relating to your course and writing assignments in particular. This might also be supplemented by references that you may be given in lectures.

Table 4.1 indicates the type of content you can expect from resources recommended in reading lists, lectures and tutorials. A preliminary internet search may help you to identify sections in a book resource or online that are also relevant to your task.

Once you have gathered the sources you intend to use, consult the contents page and the index for key headings and words as this will help you to focus your reading on a specific topic. Some authors put key pages in bold type in the index and this will help you decide on in-depth reading for your topic.

You may find that items listed on your booklist are not available on-site or electronically. This is particularly the case for journal articles because these require an institutional subscription. The precise subscriptions that libraries support will depend on factors such as the degrees taught, any teaching specialisms, the research interests of staff and past bequests or collections. The librarian with responsibility for your subject area will be able to advise you about resources available in the library or online and how to access these.

HOW TO FIND THE RESOURCES YOU NEED

Libraries use cataloguing systems to identify their resources. The system your library follows will be explained in leaflets or during a library tour. The two main possibilities are:

- **The Dewey decimal system:** here each book is given a numerical code. For example, editions of *Hamlet* by William Shakespeare are filed under 822.34.

Table 4.1 **Some of the types of content that can be obtained from library resources.** Many items are available online. For example, libraries take out subscriptions to e-book repositories, e-journals, e-newspapers and online dictionaries and encyclopaedias. Your library will have its own method of giving access to these resources, probably via the library electronic desktop. A password may be required.

Type of resource	Examples	Indication of content
Books	Prescribed texts from reading list or lectures	Provide linkage with the course content
	General textbooks	Give an overview of the subject
	Supplementary texts	Discuss the subject in greater depth
Reference books	Standard dictionaries	Provide spelling, pronunciation and meaning
	Bilingual dictionaries	Provide translation of words and expressions in two languages
	Subject-specific dictionaries	Provide definitions of key specialist terms
	General encyclopaedias	Provide a quick overview of a new topic
	Discipline-specific encyclopaedias	Provide a quick overview of specific topics
	Biographical material	Provides sources of information on key figures both contemporary and the past can be useful when beginning to study in a new area
	Yearbooks/directories	Provide up-to-date information on organisations; can be supplemented by website
	Atlases	Provide geographical or historical information
Newspapers	Daily or weekly newspapers – hard copy, online or archived	Provide coverage of contemporary issues
Periodicals and academic journals	Discipline- or subject-specific publications produced three or four times per year	Provide analysis and discussion of recent ideas, reports on current research issues
Professional journals	Specific to discipline or professional group	Provide information on recent developments in professional area
Popular periodicals	For example, *Nature, New Scientist, The Economist*	Provide coverage of emerging themes within broad fields, such as their titles suggest

- **The Library of Congress system:** here each book is given an alphanumeric code (letters and numbers). For example, editions of *Hamlet* by William Shakespeare are filed under PR2807.

Additional numbers and letters may be used to define editions and variants on a subject area. Each system may be interpreted slightly differently in different libraries. You will find the catalogue number from the library electronic catalogue. You then need to note the number and go to the appropriate shelving area in the library to locate the book.

Choosing which resources to use to gather information for your writing assignment

- Before you begin gathering your information and the resources you think you will need, consult a general or subject-specific encyclopaedia to get an overview of the topic, key issues and important contributors in the area.

- Note that you are not usually required to read all the books on a reading list. Reading lists are often compiled over years and they can grow and grow as new titles are published. Lecturers sometimes offer a number of titles covering similar ground so that all students are not trying to access the same title at the same time.

- Read only one of the recommended general texts or the coursebook (in subjects where a single text is recommended as the general text for the course). Such titles will probably be highlighted as such on your reading list. Don't waste time then reading a comparable book which will simply give you the same material merely packaged in a different way.

- Identify more specialised texts and aim to read some of these so that you begin to consider the key issues, developments, arguments or thinking that these texts detail.

- Make choices about what you read. Sometimes you may find one particular text impenetrable – boring, poorly written or unimaginatively laid out. If you feel that you cannot engage with a particular book, then find an alternative – if necessary, with help from your subject librarian. Making this kind of choice is a preliminary to the critical thinking that you will need to develop in your analysis of material content and in the writing you will produce (**Ch 11**).

How can I be more proficient when researching information and sources?

Searching for books – selecting appropriate search terms

The books on reading lists may not be available when you need them or you may feel that you want to 'think out of the box' anyway by searching for additional material yourself. This can be done in a number of ways, and your librarian will be able to help you with how to approach this as applicable to your library. However, a few tips may be useful:

Key contributors to a field – people may have contributed significantly to a field, and entering name and initials as search terms may yield a number of resources that may be useful to you. Reading some of their work may provide you with additional specialised information but also provide you with models of good writing in your field.

Names and surnames – if you have heard the name of an author only in a lecture, you may not know how their name is spelt. For example, some family names can have a number of variations – for example, *Nicol, Nicoll, Nichol*. Often the gender of an author is unknown and you need to be prepared to try 'Lesley' as well as 'Leslie' if this is used as a first name.

Search terms – be as specific as you can; sometimes search terms used are too general. For example, if you were to key in 'trees' in a catalogue search you could raise too many items with only a few relevant to your purpose. However, if you were to search under 'tree diseases' then resources relating to ash dieback and Dutch elm diseases would probably be more readily found. Sometimes the search term you have used may not be the one most commonly used in relation to your topic. For example, a search under 'prisoners' might raise details about prison conditions and nineteenth-century prisons in the UK, whereas 'hostage' as a search term using the singular form would lead you to an area about kidnapping in international law, your desired area. Therefore, looking up synonyms (words similar in meaning) can be a useful way in which to streamline your research of catalogues and search engines.

Advances in technology have meant that, through the internet, students are exposed to a vast range of resources. While this enriches understanding and potentially broadens horizons, there are some points that should be noted when accessing certain resources, especially those available online.

- Be aware that online resources may be based outside UK and so follow American English spelling and punctuation conventions. These may or may not be appropriate to writing conventions in your discipline; hence, it is advisable to ask for guidance on acceptable usage from a tutor or lecturer.

- Check that discipline-specific resources contain material that follows practices in your location. In the study of Law, for example, there are different jurisdictions with different rules.

- Online resources, for example, wikis, are not formally peer-reviewed and so their content may be unreliable.

- Reading the abstract of a journal and using that material without consulting the full article is not sufficient for academic study at university level.

- Journals and periodicals are written by academics, usually for other academic audiences. For new students, reading a lengthy journal article may be less relevant than reading a prescribed resource that lays out the fundamentals.

Using the research resources available through your library will aid your gathering of information. Having assembled a pile of books and lists of relevant URLs, you need to be able to read the material (**Ch 5**) and record key points in note form as a stage preliminary to processing the information (**Ch 6**) and producing the writing for assessment (**Chs 8–16**). Further information and tips on avoiding plagiarism and correct citation of the work of others in your text can be found in **Chapter 12**.

PRACTICAL TIPS FOR RESEARCHING INFORMATION FOR ACADEMIC PURPOSES

Find out who is the librarian with special responsibility for your subject area or module. Librarians have a wide range of knowledge about all sorts of information. If you are unsure about any aspect of the material that you will need to find through the university library, they will be able to assist you.

Be imaginative in using lateral thinking to select search terms. Not all books have titles that are as they seem, so try thinking beyond the obvious. For example, a business studies student might be covering an assignment on predatory take-over bids in the retail sector. Key words used on a catalogue search would probably have 'take-over', 'retail' or 'business' in the title. However, a search might throw up a title 'Sharks and hostile environments'. This might indeed be a book covering the predatory hunting patterns of great white sharks, but feasibly relate instead to 'sharks' in the business sense. In most instances, you can get a clue regarding the content from the catalogue number. If it has a prefix similar to other books that are on the target area, then it is likely to be useful. If the catalogue number is not similar, then the book is less likely to be relevant and, in this case, probably be related to ocean-going sharks.

Browse the journals and periodicals. Keeping up-to-date in your field is important – even for new students. Despite the increasing number of e-journals, universities still subscribe to some of the generic journals in hard copy. At points in the day when you feel that you need a break from working on your current assignment, take some time to browse the general journals that you will find in a special area within your library. These will cover issues that are topical and related to your subject in the wider sense. For example, journals such as 'Nature' and 'New Scientist' will be of interest to anyone studying in scientific subjects, whereas 'The Economist' or 'The Spectator' could be relevant to people studying in Arts and Humanities subjects. Some up-to-the-minute information you glean from such sources may provide you with examples to include in your written work.

Be wary of extending the research phase of writing indefinitely. A common strategy symptomatic of procrastination is to keep working on the literature rather than get down to writing. In planning how much time you can allocate to working on the reading of material for an assignment (**Ch 8**), accept that the priority is to submit the work on time rather than seeking an elusive 'perfect' paper or response to the task. Work to your timetable and, if a point emerges that needs supplementary reading, then you will need to factor this into your timetable. Don't be tempted to over-extend this 'extra' reading or you may fail to meet your writing deadline.

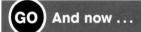 **And now ...**

4.1 Take a stroll around your university library. Finding books and other resources via the catalogue is the obvious first step in discovering what your library can provide. However, take some time out to familiarise yourself with the area where the books in your subject area are shelved. You may be surprised about what you find and so, later, be able to revisit these shelves to find books that might apply to your writing assignments but which are not on the reading list.

4.2 Find out about 'quiet' zones in your library. Some people study and write successfully with background noise, but others do not. Many libraries have areas where no mobiles, personal music players, or talking are permitted. If you prefer to work in silence, then make a point of locating the quiet zone in your library and locate some ideal spots where you would feel comfortable working.

4.3 Find out about joining the local library. Consider joining the local library in your university town. Such libraries have extensive archives of information and resources that might not be as readily available in the university library because of heavy demand from other students. The local library can often provide a 'hideaway' study location if you prefer an alternative and sometimes quieter environment than might be the case in your university library.

5

READING EFFECTIVELY

How understanding the structure of text helps your own writing

As a student, you will find that you are required to do a lot of reading when preparing to write for any sort of assignment. This chapter explains how text is structured. This has two purposes: the first is to help you read more effectively so that your understanding is improved; and the second is to help you understand the structural format you will be expected to produce in your own writing.

KEY TOPICS

→ Assessing the value of a text

→ Examining the structure of writing

→ Reading online resources

→ Checklist for evaluating your own writing

KEY UNIVERSITY TERMS

Abstract   Blurb   Discourse markers   Finger tracing   Gist
Paragraph   Sentence   Terminator paragraph   Topic paragraph
Topic sentence

Much of the material you will read as part of your studies will consist of books and journal articles (sometimes called 'papers'). These will be written following traditional academic style and, at first glance, may even appear to be heavy going. However, the academic world is particular about its conventions. By examining how printed academic resources are organised and how the text within them is structured, you should find it easier to read the pages (or screens) of print. You will gain an understanding of the content as well as save your time. Taking these texts as models will help you develop your own writing. This chapter, along with **Chapters 6** and **7**, relates to the activities involved in **Step 4** of the 12-step process to success in academic writing (**Ch 1**).

ASSESSING THE VALUE OF A TEXT

Reading is a time-consuming activity and so you will want to ensure that what you read is going to be relevant to your current task. Titles of books and journal articles can be misleading, and you will save precious time if you take a few moments to assess the validity of a resource in the context of your purpose in reading this material. You have to decide whether to investigate further; whether you need to look at the whole book, or just selected parts; or whether the book is of limited value at present. The answers to the following questions will help you to decide:

- **Title and author(s)**
  - Does this text look as though it is going to be useful to your current task?
  - Are the authors well-known authorities in the subject area?
- **Publisher's 'blurb' or abstract**
  - Does this indicate that the coverage suits your needs?
- **Publication details**
  - What is the date of publication?
  - Will this book provide you with up-to-date coverage?
  - Is this the most recent edition?
- **Contents listing (for books and reviews)**
  - Does this indicate that the book covers the key topic areas you need?
  - Do the chapter titles suggest the coverage is detailed enough?
- **Index (for books)**
  - Is this comprehensive and will it help you find what you want, quickly?
  - From a quick look, can you see references to material you want?
- **General impression**
  - Does the text look easy to read? Is the text easy to navigate via sub-headings or paragraphs?
  - Is any visual material clear and explained well?

EXAMINING THE STRUCTURE OF WRITING

Well-structured academic text usually follows a standard pattern with an introduction, main body and conclusion in each element. Sometimes the introduction may comprise several paragraphs, sometimes only one. Similarly, the conclusion may be several paragraphs or only one. Figure 5.1 shows an outline layout for a piece of text with five paragraphs, comprising an introduction and conclusion with three intervening paragraphs of varying length, each starting with a topic sentence. Note that this example is only used to illustrate the format. Normally, a written assignment would be expected to comprise more than five paragraphs.

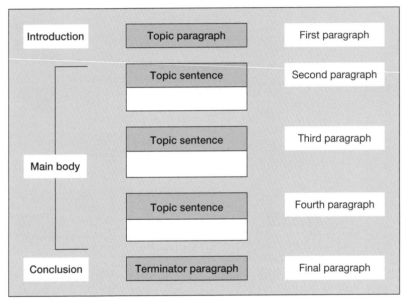

Figure 5.1 Sample textual layout in outline. You can visualise the structure of any piece of reading material in a similar fashion.

Topic sentences and paragraphs

A topic sentence is simply one that introduces the subject of a paragraph. It is normally the first sentence in the paragraph (Figure 5.1 and Example 5.1)

A topic paragraph is one that introduces the subject of a piece of formal writing. It is normally the first paragraph in the text (Figure 5.1 and Example 5.1)

Example 5.1 Sample reading text. The following text might represent the introduction to a textbook on modern communications in electrical engineering, journalism, marketing or psychology. The light shaded areas indicate the topic sentences; darker shading indicates the signpost words. You can also use this text of 744 words to assess your speed of reading (**Table A1.1**).

Introduction Topic paragraph	Technological advances and skilful marketing have meant that the mobile phone has moved from being simply an accessory to a status as an essential piece of equipment. From teenagers to grandmothers, the nation has taken to the mobile phone as a constant link for business and social purposes. As a phenomenon, the ascendancy of the mobile phone, in a multitude of ways, has had a critical impact on the way people organise their lives.	Topic sentence
	Clearly, the convenience of the mobile is attractive. It is constantly available to receive or send calls. While these are not cheap, the less expensive text-message alternative provides a similar 'constant contact' facility. At a personal and social level, this brings peace of mind to parents as teenagers can locate and be located on the press of a button. However, in business terms, while it means that employees are constantly accessible and, with more sophisticated models, can access internet communications also, there is no escape from the workplace.	Topic sentence Signpost word Signpost word
	The emergence of abbreviated text-message language has wrought a change in everyday print. For example, pupils and students have been known to submit written work using text message symbols and language. Some have declared this to mark the demise of standard English. Furthermore, the accessibility of the mobile phone has become a problem in colleges and universities, where it has been known for students in examinations to use the texting facility to obtain information required.	Topic sentence Signpost word
	The ubiquity of the mobile phone has generated changes in the way that services are offered. For instance, this means that trains, buses, and restaurants have declared 'silent zones' where the mobile is not permitted to give others a rest from the 'I'm on the train' style mobile phone conversation.	Topic sentence Signpost word
Transition paragraph	While the marked increase in mobile phone sales indicates that many in the population have embraced this technology, by contrast, 'mobile' culture has not been without its critics. Real concerns have been expressed about the potential dangers that can be encountered through mobile phone use.	Topic sentence Signpost word

	One such danger is that associated with driving while speaking on a mobile. A body of case law has been accumulated to support the introduction of new legislation outlawing the use of hand-held mobile phones by drivers whilst driving. The enforcement of this legislation is virtually impossible to police and, thus, much is down to the commonsense and responsibility of drivers. Again, technology has risen to meet the contingency with the development of 'hands – free' phones which can be used while driving and without infringing the law.	Topic sentence Signpost word
	A further danger is an unseen one, namely, the impact of the radiation from mobile phones on the human brain. Research is not well advanced in this area and data related to specific absorption rates (SARs) from the use of mobile phones and its effect on brain tissue is not yet available for evaluation. Nevertheless, although this lack of evidence is acknowledged by mobile phone companies, they advise that hands-free devices reduce the SAR levels by 98%.	Topic sentence Signpost word
	Mobile phone controversy is not confined only to the potential dangers related to the units alone; some people have serious concerns about the impact mobile phone masts have on the area surrounding them. The fear is that radiation from masts could induce serious illness amongst those living near such masts. While evidence refuting or supporting this view remains inconclusive, there appears to be much more justification for concern about emissions from television transmitters and national grid pylons which emit far higher levels of electro-magnetic radiation. Yet, little correlation appears to have been made between this fundamental of electrical engineering and the technology of telecommunications.	Topic sentence Signpost word Signpost word
Conclusion **Terminator** **paragraph**	In summary, although it appears that there are enormous benefits to mobile phone users, it is clear that there are many unanswered questions about the impact of their use on individuals. At one level, these represent an intrusion on personal privacy whether as a user or as a bystander obliged to listen to multiple one-sided conversations in public places. More significantly, there is the potential for unseen damage to the health of individual users as they clamp their mobiles to their ears. Whereas the individual has a choice to use or not to use a mobile phone, people have fewer choices in relation to exposure to dangerous emissions from masts. While the output from phone masts is worthy of further investigation, it is in the more general context of emissions from electro-magnetic masts of all types that serious research needs to be developed.	Topic sentence Signpost word Signpost word Signpost word Signpost word

Within the structure of the text, each paragraph will be introduced by a topic sentence stating the content of the paragraph. Each paragraph thereafter performs a function. For example, some may describe, others may provide examples, while others may examine points in favour of a particular position and others points against that position.

The function of these paragraphs, and the sentences within them, is usually signalled by use of 'signpost words' guiding the reader through the logical structure of the text. For example, the word 'however' indicates that some contrast is going to be made with a point immediately before; 'therefore' or 'thus' signal that a result or effect is about to be explained. Further examples of signpost words are given in **Table 16.2**. Use of such words in your own writing will contribute to the logic of your argument.

Example 5.1 shows a sample text in which all the elements mentioned here are illustrated.

From the 'deconstruction' of text in Figure 5.1 and Example 5.1, the skeletal structure of academic text becomes more apparent. You can use this knowledge to establish the substance of a piece of text by:

● reading the topic and terminator paragraphs, or even just their topic sentences, to gain a quick overview of the direction taken by the writer

● scanning through the text for key words related to your focus. This scanning may indicate particular paragraphs worthy of detailed reading. Sometimes headings and sub-headings may be used, which will facilitate a search of this kind

● looking for signpost words to indicate the text and how its underlying 'argument' is organised.

These approaches can help you to become a more efficient reader. Find out about speed reading and how to calculate your reading speed in **Appendix 1**.

READING ONLINE RESOURCES

You can always print out material sourced from the internet, in which case, similar principles apply to those described elsewhere in this chapter. However, due to cost as well as environmental considerations, or simply the fact that you have to assess the material before committing yourself to a printout, you may prefer to read directly from the screen. The following points need to be taken into consideration in such instances:

- web page designers often divide text into screen-sized chunks, with links between pages. This can make it difficult to gain an overall picture of the topic being covered. Make sure that you read through all the material before forming a judgement about it

- one benefit of web-based material is that it is often written in a 'punchy' style, with bulleted lists and easily assimilated 'take home' messages, often highlighted with graphics. This may mean that the content lacks the detail required for academic work, for example, in the number and depth of examples given

- the ease of access of web-based materials might cause a bias in your reading – perhaps towards more modern sources, but also, potentially, away from the overtly academic. Always check to see whether 'standard' printed texts are advised on reading lists or are available in your library. If so, you should consult these as well as web-based material

- the act of skimming text (see **Appendix 1**) can be accelerated by using the 'find' function (control + F in MS Word and Internet Explorer) to skip to key words

- if you do decide to print out a resource, check on the screen for an icon that might give you a 'printer friendly' version.

CHECKLIST FOR EVALUATING YOUR OWN WRITING

As a reader, you may find that it is often easier to critique the writing of others than your own. Taking the ideas outlined in this chapter, you can now develop a strategy for 'decoding' the logic of extensive and even complex texts written by others. This will help you to understand content and so consciously assess what you read.

By contrast, thinking of yourself in the role of author as well as reader can be helpful. As writers, we are sometimes too 'close' to the writing to be able to see its flaws. The same strategies that you used for assessing the structure of what you read can be applied to assess the construction of your own writing. In this way you will be more able to recognise structural weaknesses. To do this, you should consider the following aspects:

- **Introduction**
    - Does this encapsulate the theme in the topic sentence(s)?
    - Does it succinctly explain what is to follow and why?
- **Main body**
    - Are the paragraphs well-structured and of appropriate length?
    - Does each paragraph encapsulate a 'unit' of information or discussion?
    - Do the paragraphs introduce content and conclude by providing transition to the next paragraph?
    - Is it possible to group some paragraphs together as sharing a particular aspect of discussion?
- **Logic**
    - Can the reader easily identify the key arguments or points and see these reflected in the conclusion?
- **Language**
    - Does the writer help to structure points by use of signpost words such as those listed in **Table 16.2**?
    - Does the writer explain specialist terms?
    - Are grammatically allied words and specialised terms used and are these explained well?

Thus, as an academic author you will be finding ways of presenting your own ideas clearly and logically. This will help your own reader (often 'the marker') to decode and evaluate your written text.

 PRACTICAL SKILLS FOR READING EFFECTIVELY

Choose reading material that suits your learning style. Sometimes reading lists offer a number of alternative sources of material. If you find that the writing style or the format of one of these books is not to your taste, then look for an alternative from the reading list or from the library catalogue. Finding material presented in ways that complement your learning style (**Ch 6**) can be enlightening and help you to understand the content more readily.

Use publication dates as guides to appropriate source material. Finding material by title using the library catalogue is relatively easy. However, you still have to make some critical choices about what you find there. Look for the date of publication – in the book itself, this will usually be on the left-hand page after the title page. You should try to obtain the most recent edition of the resource as this will have revisions of fact, data or perspective that may have altered since earlier editions were published.

Take regular breaks. Unlike reading fiction where the storyline carries the reader along, academic texts can be more demanding. Every paragraph, every sentence and even every word can be laden with meaning that requires concentration on the whole as well as the individual elements. Therefore, it is better to split up your reading so that you take a break at a logical stopping point, for example, at the end of a section or chapter. You will return to the task with fresh energy and perhaps with better understanding as the ideas have had time to settle in your mind.

(GO) And now ...

5.1 Monitor your reading speed if you feel that this is limiting your progress. Consult the guidance given in **Appendix 1** on speed-reading. Take a suitable text to work from and calculate your reading speed. After a period of a couple of weeks using the reading methods recommended, and deciding which suits you best, check your reading speed to see if you have improved.

5.2 Practise surveying a text using a book from your reading list. Rather than simply reading the prescribed pages, spend five or ten minutes beforehand looking through the contents page and the text itself. Think about how the author has organised the content and why. Does the author provide an introduction that gives an overview of the book and would this be worth skim-reading to achieve a better understanding of the prescribed pages later in the book? Does the final chapter provide a review of the key issues covered in the book and, again, would this be worth skim-reading as a summary that would help your understanding?

5.3 Expand your vocabulary to help develop your academic writing. Particularly if you are new to an area of study or topic, you may find that some of the technical language is new to you. A subject-specific dictionary can be a useful asset but you may also find that some of the prescribed textbooks contain glossary pages that can be of assistance. However, specialist terms represent only a fraction of academic text. The non-specialist words are the 'glue' that sticks it all together so that it makes sense. This can mean that students find non-specialist words in their reading that are unknown or unfamiliar, as used in the specialist context. Make a point of looking up such words in a good dictionary. Note their meaning and usage so that you can expand your understanding and introduce some of this new language into your own writing.

6

NOTES FROM LECTURES AND READING

How to record information in note form for use in your writing

Keeping a record of what you hear in lectures and what you read in the literature contribute to the development of your own academic writing skills. The activity of processing information is a useful preparation for writing for assessment. This chapter outlines practical ways in which you can keep a record of what you hear and read in appropriate note form so that it is meaningful to you when preparing written work.

KEY TOPICS

→ Why notes are important as an input to your writing

→ What good notes should contain

→ Note-taking and note-making with purpose

→ How are you going to lay out your notes?

KEY UNIVERSITY TERMS

Annotate   Authorities   Copyright   Literature   Mnemonic
Recto   Verbatim   Verso

The skill of creating notes is a key element of **Step 4** in the 12-step process of academic writing (**Table 1.1**). You will develop this skill as you progress in your studies, but it will take time and experimentation to achieve methods that suit you best. There are several methods from which you can choose to record key points of content from both lectures and literature.

WHY NOTES ARE IMPORTANT AS AN INPUT TO YOUR WRITING

As a student, you will receive information through a variety of media. Your job is to gather and organise this information in ways that are meaningful, logical and retrievable. If your notes are chaotic (or non-existent), then you will be unlikely to achieve good writing. Essentially, there are two situations where recording information is important:

1 in listening mode, that is, in a lecture (or tutorial or lab) where you will be **taking** notes under time pressure (**Ch 3**) or

2 in researching/reading mode where you are **making** notes at your own speed from what you read (**Ch 4** and **Ch 5**).

The essential difference relating to notes in these two contexts is that, in a listening situation, you are taking notes spontaneously based on the interpretation offered by the speaker, organised in ways that fit their logic and sequenced within the time constraints of the listening episode. By contrast, in a reading mode, you are the person 'in control'. Hence, you are making notes reflectively based on your interpretation of the text and framed in a format that suits your logic, your purpose in recording information and within your own time constraints. In both instances, how you create notes will reflect your learning style.

 What are learning styles?

How you learn best is dictated by your natural preferences for handling new, unfamiliar information. Some people prefer to learn by using visual influences, some prefer aural explanations to written ones, others prefer to read and write to aid their learning and a further category prefer to use all their senses to experience learning. These types can be listed as **V**isual, **A**ural, **R**ead-write and **K**inesthetic. These terms are used by the New Zealand academic, Neil Fleming, to explain learning styles. His VARK website at www.vark-learn.com/english/index.asp provides opportunities to complete a simple questionnaire that suggests the learning style that is nearest to your own learning preferences.

WHAT GOOD NOTES SHOULD CONTAIN

Whatever the situation, you need to be clear about the reasons for creating the notes. These will influence their style, detail and depth. For example, if your notes are to support your revision, they will tend to be more detailed overall. If your notes aim to collate material for writing an assignment, they may be more focussed on specific aspects. Table 6.1 identifies typical reasons for creating notes according to whether you are listening or reading. This contrasts the spontaneity of notes taken in lectures – often resulting in less detailed or incomplete notes, with notes from texts made under less pressure – so allowing time for reflection and deeper understanding.

The high quality notes you create from lectures or from texts will help considerably when you use them to draft your writing. Good notes should:

- contain accurate information about source material
- include verbatim quotes where appropriate (but identify them clearly as such)
- aid understanding of complex issues

Table 6.1 **Reasons for recording information in note form as an input to your understanding and subsequent writing.**

Reasons for taking lecture notes	Reasons for making notes from texts
• Obtain an outline or overview for the subject as interpreted by the lecturer/speaker	• Construct a framework or overview for the subject via general textbook resources
• Recall expert's interpretation of major points, factors, issues, controversies, problems	• Examine specialist texts for detail e.g. Sequences or processes; analysis of issues, controversies or problems
• Record oral explanation introducing or enhancing complex material by simplifying through practical or topical examples	• Extract the logic of an argument comparing and contrasting different perspectives or authorities
• Identify work of key research(ers) and provide analysis	• Isolate relevant quotes (with suitable citation (**Ch 12**)
• Note guidance on in-depth follow-up research/reading	• Allow addition of your own commentary on topic, perhaps by linking key points with what has been discussed in lecture or tutorial

- allow comparison and contrast between literature sources and in relationship to lecture input (as appropriate)
- save time in relocating source material
- include your own additional thoughts and ideas in response to the input information you have heard or researched.

NOTE-TAKING AND NOTE-MAKING WITH PURPOSE

In lectures, creating notes needs to be quick and often 'dirty' in that these are usually less organised than you might have chosen if you were looking at printed text on screen or in a hard copy book or journal. Thus, you may need to compromise neatness and structure for content:

- identify and list the aims (declared purpose) of the lecture numerically and try to identify and note the details of these aspects as they come up in the lecture
- be selective in what you write down – trying to write every word (*verbatim* notes) is impossible – you'll miss out on understanding ideas, explanations and examples
- listen for sense – people often do not speak in full sentences and so repetition, pausing and 'false starts' have to be taken into account when filtering out what you note
- listen for and note the key ideas (**Ch 3**)
- listen for the signpost words (**Table 16.2**) – these might indicate transition from one point to the next, for example, expressions, such as 'firstly, secondly …', 'however' and 'to summarise'. These will possibly signify a new element or direction in your notes
- listen for references to relevant reading texts – these may only be given as the author surname and the year of the publication. Highlight these references for follow-up action on your part.

From reading, as noted in **Chapter 5**, most courses provide a reading list of recommended resources. In addition, you may be expected to undertake further research and reading on your own initiative. The techniques described in **Chapter 5** will help you to identify the most relevant parts of the text quickly and so provide basic information for your notes. Nevertheless, sometimes students see note-making as a chore which has to be completed rather than an activity where they are engaged with the content. Consequently, the making of notes can become a re-write of the printed text. This is time-consuming and pointless. By consciously deciding on the reason for the note-taking and adopting a style that is suited to that situation, you are more likely to be reading with purpose, you will save time and produce a resource that will contribute usefully to your draft writing. For example:

1 identify your purpose in relation to the assignment or task you have to fulfil and anticipate the most appropriate layout or approach in this instance

2 scan the section to be read

3 establish the writer's purpose, for example:

 – a narrative of events or a process

 – a statement of facts

 – an explanation of reasoning or presentation of a logical argument

4 work out their 'take' on the subject and how this relates to your purpose

5 review your decision on the most appropriate note-making style and layout for your notes; amend in the light of assessing the content of the text explained in previous chapters

6 ensure you paraphrase using your own words rather than transcribe; but, if you do transcribe, use quotation marks ('…') and note reference detail

7 follow stages 1–3 of the SQ3R method (Table 6.2) to allow you to:

 – judge whether the printed sources you have obtained are simply 'dip in and out', while others will require intensive reading

 – obtain a clear idea of what is covered in the content before making notes in one of the styles outlined in **Figures A2.1– A2.7**. By doing so, you will avoid wasting time struggling with understanding the content and possibly resorting to copying out the text *verbatim*.

Practical hints for creating notes

■ **Save time when filing your notes** – number the pages of your notes and always record full details of the source:
- Lecturer/author surname and initials
- Title of lecture/chapter
- Date of lecture or publication of text
- Publisher and place of publication (in the case of literature only)

For lectures, this information will be helpful in guiding your reading and structuring your revision. For books, you will need these details to enable you to cite the source of information in your own writing (**Ch 12**).

■ **Cultivate your own 'code' for later interpretation** – for example:
- Underlining or highlighting points emphasised by the lecturer
- Asterisks (*) for points or new words to look up later
- BLOCK CAPITALS for sub-headings or keywords
- Special abbreviations for your subject that are in general use or that you create for yourself
- A symbol (e.g. #) that indicates your thought or response to a point made by the lecturer
- Colour coding
- Numbered lists
- Mnemonics
- Boxes for important points

■ **Use white space** – don't cram as much information as you can onto a sheet; leave white space around lists or other important items of information. By using the 'visual' part of your brain, you will recall information more easily. This additional space can be used if you wish to add further detail later.

■ **Develop a personal style** – ensure that your note-taking and note-making styles provide you with notes that will be meaningful in six days, weeks or months (**Figures A2.1–A2.7**).

■ **Make your notes memorable** – it is important to make sure that your notes are legible and memorable. However, spending lots of time to make them look pretty will not necessarily pay dividends. Again, try to achieve a balance – visually memorable enough to trigger your recall but not so elaborate that it becomes a meaningless work of art without substance.

What is the best way to create electronic notes in lectures?

Modern technological aids such as tablets or electronic notebooks have the potential to be convenient and effective, especially those whose handwriting is slow or illegible.

If you opt to take notes using such devices, then you will need to evolve strategies that will allow you to type up what you want to record in real time – assuming that your typing skills are good, then you might be able to do this. However, the relative limitations of the screen may restrict layout possibilities. To optimise your ability to record key points, a useful strategy might be to create a template to allow you to follow the keyword note style shown in hand-written form in Figure A2.1 in **Appendix 2**. A table structure might look like:

Lecture title:		Lecturer:	Date
Keyword	Notes relating to key word		
"	"		
"	"		
"	"		

This will enable you to use the tab key to shift quickly from keyword to note content without having to format text. Note, however, that typing within tables can present other problems such as formatting. Therefore, experimenting with this technique will be necessary before you find a system that works well for you.

While, undoubtedly, there are advantages in taking notes electronically, there are also disadvantages. The most significant is that lecture note-taking is a skill that develops the ability to write quickly under stress. By relying on the keyboard rather than the pen, students may find that they lose (or never develop) their ability to write at speed. Without the essential practice in handwriting, your ability to write by hand 'against the clock' in exams could be critically impaired.

Should I re-write my lecture notes?

A key dilemma to be confronted by any student engaged in note-taking and note-making is to decide whether the time spent on note creation is worthwhile.

In relation to lecture notes, many students spend hours copying out lecture notes. Several questions arise. Is this done to:

1 make notes more legible?
2 aid understanding?
3 help learn the content?
4 have a resource for revision?
5 record the views of lecturing staff in order to echo these in assignments and exam answers?

Positive responses to questions 1–4 are arguably acceptable, but a positive response to question 5 would be unsafe since the object of the lecture is not to provide 'ready-made' answers. Furthermore, in many cases, there are no 'right/wrong' answers. Lectures are used to introduce content, problems, viewpoints and analysis for consideration. Lecturers will expect to see your own interpretation supported your own logical argument and evidence in your writing. They will not wish to read a 're-hash' of their own lecture material that shows no evidence of understanding beyond what has been heard. This strategy will lead to very low grades for assessed writing.

A better strategy, in the first instance, might be to adopt a lecture note-taking style that is legible and as coherent as possible (given that lecturers notoriously jump around in presenting their ideas). Additionally, write notes only on one side of the paper (*recto* – the right hand sheet when your file is opened) and use the left hand (*verso*) sheet to annotate your notes by listing key points distilled from the information you took down in the lecture and using the strategies suggested in the Tip Box giving 'Practical hints creating notes'.

Would it not save time to photocopy or scan text?

Sometimes you may find that the extent of notes you require is minimal, or that a particular book or other resource is in high demand and has been placed on short-loan in the Library. It may be convenient to photocopy or scan the relevant pages, which can then be highlighted and annotated. Remember that there are restrictions imposed on the amount you can copy under copyright law – details will be posted prominently in your library. However, note that as a learning technique this type of activity is essentially passive, and, if your note-making is meant as an aid for writing, memorising or revising, one of the more active methods described in this chapter may be better.

HOW ARE YOU GOING TO LAY OUT YOUR NOTES?

How you create notes, whether in lectures or from reading, will reflect your learning style, the time that you can allocate to the task and what is best suited to the material and the subject area you are considering.

Some techniques may seem better suited to lectures rather than recording the literature, and some may not seem directly suitable to your subject or learning style or they may simply not work for you. Table 6.2 provides an analysis of the relative advantages and disadvantages of the seven examples of note-creation shown as Figures A2.1–A2.7 in **Appendix 2**.

Finally, in relation to notes and writing, notes should be recognised as resources and the time you spend creating and annotating them is an investment for learning and revising as well as for writing. They should not be thrown away. You may need to refer back to your notes as they represent the input to your understanding. What you discounted in early planning and drafting of your writing may transpire to be relevant later in the writing process. If you have discarded your notes, then you may have to spend precious time trying to re-locate and re-read the source material.

Table 6.2 A comparison of seven methods of note-creation. These are illustrated as Figures A2.1–A2.7 in **Appendix 2**.

Note type	Example	Advantage	Disadvantage
Keyword notes	Figure A2.1	Good as a layout for easy access to information; clearly demarcated aspects	Dependent on systematic structure in lecture/text
Linear notes	Figure A2.2	Numbered sequence – good for classifying ideas and for analysis, especially from texts	Restrictive format, difficult to back-track to insert new information in lectures
Time lines	Figure A2.3	Sequences events or stages in a process. Assists in narrative writing	Limited information possible; less useful for analytical writing
Flow-chart notes	Figure A2.4	Allows clear path through complex options; favours sequential narrative in writing	Takes up space; may be unwieldy
Concept maps/ Mind maps/ Explosion charts	Figure A2.5	Good for recording information on a single page; allows overview and aids analysis for planning writing	Can become messy; can be difficult to follow; not suited to all learning styles; needs to be synthesised for planning writing
Matrix notes/ Grid notes	Figure A2.6	Good layout for recording different viewpoints, approaches, applications; good for producing analysis and evaluation in writing	Space limitations on content or amount of information
Herring-bone diagrams	Figure A2.7	Good for laying opposing sides of an argument; good for visual learners when planning writing	Space limitations on content or amount of information

Note-making formats

Sometimes notes may be better suited to being laid out on paper in the landscape rather than the portrait orientation. This clearly suits methods such as concept maps (Figure A2.5 in **Appendix 2**). Similarly, you can take advantage of the landscape format when making matrix (grid) notes (Figure A2.6 in **Appendix 2**) by creating columns across the page.

PRACTICAL TIPS FOR CREATING NOTES FROM LECTURES AND READING

Go to the lecture with the right equipment. Make sure that you take your own paper, folders and writing materials, as well as calculators (if appropriate) to your lectures. It is best to use A4 paper rather than the smaller A5 reporters' notebooks. It may seem more convenient to carry a smaller pad, but the pages will be too small for your lecture notes and won't file well alongside handouts that are usually A4 in size. If you have opted to take notes electronically, then ensure that your computer is sufficiently charged for the duration of the lecture. Always back up relevant files frequently.

Keep thinking about the content as you hear or read it. The strategies suggested in this chapter for creating notes should help you keep on track with the lecture or text you are reading. However, sometimes fatigue or lack of attention can take over and notes are made 'on autopilot'. If this becomes the case for you in a lecture, put your pen down and listen intently to the lecturer rather than try to take notes that are going to be meaningless. After a few moments, once you have picked up the sense again, return to note-taking. In the case of note-making from reading that has become mechanical, stop reading and take a break – move around or go for a walk. Even five minutes away from the desk will help you to adjust your concentration. However, it is probably advisable to revisit the most recent notes you have made and refine them so that they gain some focus on the topic.

Develop your own 'shorthand'. Some subjects have their own abbreviations, for example, MI (myocardial infarction) or WTO (World Trade Organisation), and, of course, there are standard abbreviations – e.g., i.e., etc. However, you will also find it useful to develop your own abbreviations and symbols, drawn from your own experience, for example, maths symbols, text messaging or words from other languages. As long as these are memorable and meaningful to you, then they can be useful tools in making and taking notes.

GO And now . . .

6.1 Experiment with different styles of notes. Lecturers and authors differ in the way that they present information to their listeners and readers. This means that the style of notes you elect to create should be a response to these different methods of information delivery. Sometimes keeping track of a lecture that has many digressions may mean that you adopt a mind-map rather than a linear note format; similarly, a complex text may be easier to understand and record in a grid format. Only by experimenting with the different techniques shown in **Appendix 2** will you be able to identify methods that suit you and the material best.

6.2 Find out about abbreviations. Find a general dictionary that gives a comprehensive list of abbreviations and identify ones that you might use; find a specialist dictionary and identify whether it provides a list of specialist abbreviations. This will mean that you will know where to look if you come across an abbreviation that is unfamiliar to you.

6.3 Compare notes with those of a friend. Students often assume that there is only one interpretation of a lecture or text. If you and a friend exchange your notes relating to the same material, you may be surprised to find that your perceptions about emphasis and relative merits of an issue differ. This should lead to fruitful, perhaps heated, discussion about the content. You may also learn from the format and style that you have chosen to use in creating these notes.

7

SPEAKING, THINKING AND ACADEMIC WRITING

How discussing your work contributes to organising and wording your writing

Speaking is a way of expressing ideas, thoughts, opinions and much more. When speaking about your work, you will be 'rehearsing' the word patterns and the use of specialist terminology as well as organising your thoughts, structuring and evaluating argument. This chapter examines ways in which informal and formal speaking contribute to writing.

KEY TOPICS

→ Speaking in informal situations

→ Speaking in formal situations

KEY UNIVERSITY TERMS

Vernacular   *Vice versa*

Speaking and writing are interlinked. The one can be the preliminary for the other and *vice versa.* What is said in a lecture, for example, usually begins its journey to oral explanation as a piece of text. What is written in formal print is often the product, not just of mental processing but also of oral expression. As a student, you may be required to speak in both informal and formal situations – less formal discussions can take place in tutorials and labs, whereas more formal oral contributions may be required in lectures and debate. In each case, speaking will assist you in shaping your writing and the aspects covered in this chapter contribute to **Step 4** in the 12-step process of writing (**Table 1.1**).

SPEAKING IN INFORMAL SITUATIONS

Speaking and its companion, listening, are vital elements in gathering and processing information. As a speaker, when you articulate ideas, you may be passing on information or contributing to a debate, for example. As a listener, for example, in a tutorial, you gain from the insights and perspectives of others and add these to your own mental processes.

However, before you open your mouth to initiate a theme within a discussion or to react to what you have heard, you need to make a mental or written note of the points that you want to make and place them in a logical sequence so that your contribution is cogent and well-expressed. This will give you confidence to speak and also ensure that people listen more closely to your points. How you speak and the impact of your contribution will enhance the perception of others about your ability to frame your ideas well.

Watch how politicians, interviewers and spokespersons deal with questions or present information or viewpoints. Whether this is done well or badly, you may pick up some tips that will help you to present your own ideas and avoid pitfalls in discussion.

Even in informal situations, avoid slang and sloppy pronunciation. Others may not understand your particular vernacular and may misunderstand the points you are trying to make.

 Expressing your ideas in front of others

Many people are often reluctant to speak in public or even offer an opinion in less formals situations. Students often have reservations about expressing their ideas even within smallish groups. University is a place where you will be expected at least to make some sort of contribution to discussion, for example, in tutorial, seminar, lab, workshop, practical or moot (in Law) sessions. You may find that in some courses your contributions will be included as part of the course assessment. Try not to shy away from putting your thoughts into words. Your ideas are as worth airing as anyone else's; explaining your ideas is part of your academic training. Speaking about your views and thoughts will help you to structure your argument or supporting evidence logically and succinctly. In addition, you may receive helpful, constructive feedback on these from your lecturer or others in the group.

How to 'get in' to a discussion

Learning the conventions and courtesies of discussion is a useful communication skill that is life-long. Where you want to contribute to an informal or a formal discussion, then look to the 'chair' or person leading the discussion – often the lecturer or tutor, although a fellow student may have been tasked with leading the discussion. You can draw attention to yourself by making eye contact or raising a pen to show that you wish to speak. You will then probably be invited to speak. Formulating what you want to say in a written note first of all will ensure that you express yourself clearly and without stumbling.

SPEAKING IN FORMAL SITUATIONS

Speaking in formal situations is something that takes time and experimentation to perfect. The key lies in preparation. This means that you need to construct the oral presentation in written format. You will need to begin with a plan that leads to the production of a script and then distillation to cue cards (if that is how you wish to make your presentation).

The steps that you need to follow in planning and writing your presentation are:

1 identify why you are doing the presentation, for example,
   - for assessment
   - for passing on an idea
   - for passing on new information
2 consider the context, for example,
   - the area of study
   - the set topic
3 decide what you are trying to do, for example,
   - describing a development or process
   - explaining an approach
   - presenting a viewpoint
4 brainstorm for content, bearing in mind context and purpose(s)

5 decide on a structure for delivery of your material by deciding what to include/exclude

6 taking the level and composition of the audience into account and the time at your disposal, plan the key points and order them as a logical progression of your explanation or argument

7 develop each of your key points by providing reasoned argument with supporting evidence or data in the form of results or figures

8 draw up a list of your conclusions with a brief explanation

9 list any recommendations (as appropriate) providing rationale for each

10 write a short summary or brief review of each point

11 separate your presentation into sections – possibly as simply as Introduction, Main body and Conclusion. Within these sections, distil your script into headings with subsidiary points that will provide the cues for you to use in the presentation

12 practise the oral delivery using your cue card prompts so that you can time the length of the presentation and adjust according to the time you are allocated. Bear in mind that, when nervous, people usually speak faster than they perhaps might when practising. You may need to make a conscious effort to maintain an even pace in line with the pace that you followed when practising.

This 12-stage approach depends on written preparation and, in some ways, replicates the processes that you need to go through in preparing a first draft of assessed formal writing. Unlike formal written assessments that are often only ever seen by the author and the person grading them, the spoken presentation is a situation where your abilities are on display to listeners – your peers and academic staff. This means that clear planning and writing are essential for success; your writing ability is as necessary for spoken presentations as it is for written assignments.

PRACTICAL TIPS FOR SPEAKING, THINKING AND ACADEMIC WRITING

Identify role models who speak well about your subject. People whom you encounter – lectures, tutors, demonstrators, postgraduate students – all have something to offer you in the way that they speak about their subject. In the course of talking formally or informally, they will provide you with ways of explaining and giving examples as well as the use of language that is the norm for your discipline. Picking up on these conventions will help you speak in an informed way within your academic community and this should transfer to your writing.

Make the links between speaking, thinking and writing. In participating in discussion about a topic, there is a need to formulate what you want to say. This involves thinking through ideas and, as discussion continues, further thoughts will come to mind. Thinking is a preliminary to speaking and, as with writing, sometimes the thinking goes on while the speaking or writing is actually happening. It is wise to recognise that this happens and note down some of these transient or unexpected thoughts as a contribution to your information gathering.

Ensure that you can be heard. For most people, the norm is to use their voices in conversational contexts. Apart perhaps from shouting on a team or trying to attract someone's attention at a distance, the opportunities to raise your voice may have been limited. In academic contexts, you may have to speak in situations where the room is large and the listeners are many. Even the best prepared oral input to a debate or presentation will be irrelevant if other participants cannot hear you. If you feel that your voice will not 'carry', then work with friends by practising projecting your voices in large spaces. Some strategies you might try include:

1 asking some friends to sit at the back of a room or lecture theatre as others take turns to practise speeches or presentations.

   - If speakers are not heard clearly, listeners can use hand signals to indicate that voices need to be raised or lowered.

   - If speakers are talking too quickly, then hand signals can be used in a similar way to indicate that the speaker needs to slow down or speed up.

2 at the time of the presentation, arrange for a friend to sit near the back of the room so that, using hand signals, they can indicate from there whether you need to speak more loudly or more slowly.

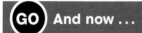 **And now ...**

7.1 Attend lectures given by visiting experts to learn about good presentation and explanation. People who are invited to speak in public lectures or are hosted as visiting lecturers are usually invited to do so because they are excellent speakers as well as respected researchers. Apart from attending such lectures for the content, observe some of the techniques that experts use to talk about their subject and explain their work – remember that this will stem from their own writing.

7.2 Watch television discussion programmes to learn about how to participate in debate. Programmes of this type can lead to energetic discussion on the debating topic. Make a point of noting how successful contributions to the debate are made. This will involve listening for language devices used to get into the debate (for example, *'I have three points I'd like to make'*) and watching for body language such as leaning forward or pushing the hand sideways on to the table to indicate that the person has something to say. Learning from these programmes will enable you to feel more confident about contributing to informal and formal discussions.

7.3 Take action to develop your public speaking skills. If you feel that you lack confidence about speaking in front of others or do not like speaking in public, then take positive steps to get yourself over this hurdle. For example:

- search out a local Speakers' Club and learn from experts in a fun and non-threatening way.

- join a debating society and volunteer to stand in debate on a subject about which you are passionate. Your detailed preparation and enthusiasm for the topic plus the inevitable adrenalin rush will carry you over your reservations.

- involve yourself in student representation at class or Student Union level where you will have opportunities to engage in speaking in more formal contexts. As well as involving you in responsible decision-making, this will help you to become a confident contributor to discussions and presentations.

Preparing for such activities will help you to formulate your ideas in written format in the first instance and this will influence later writing for assignments.

UNDERSTANDING THE CONTEXTS AND PRACTICES RELATING TO ACADEMIC WRITING

- HOW TO MEET THE STANDARDS

8

ORGANISING YOURSELF FOR WRITING

How to use your time
effectively to ensure successful
completion of assignments

Time is of the essence in the process of writing for academic
purposes. It can be wasted, or simply evaporate, because of lack
of personal organisation. Inevitably, this jeopardises the quality of
the writing product. This chapter suggests ways in which you can
take control of any writing task and so overcome procrastination,
disorganisation and lack of understanding about how to focus on the
job in hand.

KEY TOPICS

→ Being realistic about time

→ The sequence of work and planning your time

→ Initial phase of gathering information

→ Working from the material

KEY UNIVERSITY TERMS

Aspect   Restriction   Virtual learning environment (VLE)

Planning for writing involves more than planning the way that you put
your writing together. It involves a considerable amount of personal
organisation so that you are able to work within limits of time,
availability and location. This means that your first task is to work out
your timetable according to a number of stages in the process. This
chapter lays out a template that can help you follow a logical path
to achieve completion and in particular introduces ways in which to
analyse the task you have been set.

BEING REALISTIC ABOUT TIME FOR WRITING

A piece of academic writing is usually lengthy and complex, although you may find that a word-limit is imposed on your submission. Therefore, completing a piece of writing for assessment is not something that can be achieved in a brief interlude between lectures, work or social activities. It takes time and you need to be realistic about just how much time it will take within the parameters of time you have available.

The first thing – **Step 1** in the 12-step writing process – is to establish how much time lies between starting and submission dates. You'll find this in your course handbook (**Table 1.1**). To plan time effectively, you need to take into account how many other things you need to fit around working on the assignment – lectures, tutorials, labs, work for other modules or subjects, family, social or employment commitments.

 Value of planning

Time spent deconstructing the task and planning your response will enable you to save time in the long run and, as with most jobs, the quality of the preparation will be reflected in the quality of the end-product. Take time to break down the question into its different elements. Good planning ensures that you can realistically complete work before the submission date. It also allows you to balance the time spent on different components, devote sufficient time to aspects such as editing and proof-reading and avoid penalties that might be imposed because of late submission. It also means that your essay won't be a 'last minute' effort that will lack logic, accuracy and analysis.

THE SEQUENCE OF WORK AND PLANNING YOUR TIME

As we noted in **Chapter 1**, in general terms, the 12-step process for successful academic writing involves certain generic phases that you need to take into account to plan your work. These are:

- gathering information
- processing information
- creating the text
- developing future writing

Table 8.1 shows that there is some overlap where gathering information, at some points, runs alongside processing information. Similarly, processing information continues through a significant part of the creating text phase. In terms of the 12-step approach, these follow a logical sequence within the overlapping phases: **Steps 1 to 5** involve information gathering (**Chs 2–7**), but **Steps 2 to 9** encompass various aspects of information processing (**Chs 8–14**), overlapping with **Steps 6 to 10** of the final writing output (**Chs 15–17**). The final stages (**Steps 11–12**) relate to post-submission action and to developing your writing for future assignments and exams (**Chs 18–19**).

Breaking academic writing activities into these four phases and their associated steps can help you with planning your time so that you complete the work by the set deadline. Decide how much time you wish to allocate to each of these aspects of the task and map these allowances on to the available time. You may find it useful to complete a table like this to help you to organise your time when planning a lengthy written assignment and so keep on track. These principles of planning hold good for revision and timing writing in exams.

INITIAL PHASE OF GATHERING INFORMATION

Once you have worked out the time allocation for the work, no time should be lost in getting down to the task of information gathering:

- **Step 1** – consult handbook for task information

  Obtain the information about your writing assignment from the handbook (**Ch 2**)

- **Step 2** – identify recommended material

  Locate the relevant recommended reading should be easily accomplished by consulting your handbook or course area on your virtual learning environment (**Ch 2**).

- **Step 3** – research and obtain relevant material

  This step involves trawling your library catalogue and shelves will probably be more protracted than Steps 1 and 2 (**Ch 4**).

- **Step 4** – read the material

  Chapters 2–7 outlined the contribution that reading, listening and speaking make to your understanding and ultimately your writing. **Chapter 6** specifically deals with effective ways for creating notes in preparation for producing academic writing.

Table 8.1 Allocating time to the 12-step approach to academic writing.
This table provides a template to allow you to estimate the timing of the stages to achieve successful completion of the set task.

	Subdivisions	Typical actions	Time set aside	Target finish date
Gathering information	**Step 1** Consult course or module handbook	• verify assignment dates • analyse nature and wording of assignment • note learning outcomes for the assignment		
	Step 2 Identify relevant/ recommended material	• create lecture/tutorial/ lab notes • consult reading list and any in-lecture references		
	Step 3 Research/obtain material	• access source material via on-site library or online		
Processing information	**Step 4** Read material	• frame notes for relevance to assignment		
	Step 5 Analyse wording of assignment	• identify what you are being instructed to do		
	Step 6 Reflect on the topic	• evaluate the response that you will construct		
Creating text	**Step 7** Plan your writing	• ensure good fit with standard framework		
	Step 8 Create a first draft	• shape your academic writing style; use critical thinking and avoid plagiarism		
	Step 9 Finalise reference list	• construct the list of supporting materials as you write		
	Step 10 Review text for submission	• edit and proof-read		
Developing future writing	**Step 11** Consider feedback	• assess how to modify content and technique for inclusion in your future written assignments		
	Step 12 Modify academic writing for exam conditions	• use feedback to contribute to revision and to adjust writing for exam purposes		

Keeping on track

Having worked out your timetable, you need to make sure that you follow it. You need to be firm with yourself so that you do not over-run the time allocation in certain areas. For example, close to the end of the process, students of every level are often found to be looking for 'just one more book' in the hope that it will provide that extra piece of information that will push up the grade on the work. It is better to draw a mental line and work with the material you have and apply this to your own thinking and analysis of the issues. If you 'overspend' time on collecting the material, then that will reduce the time that you can spend on other aspects of producing the final copy to a good standard.

WORKING FROM THE MATERIAL

After **Step 4**, the main activity of gathering information normally gives way entirely to processing information, although you may find that you revisit the resources at later points to confirm facts or find new information. When processing information, you need to apply your understanding of your reading to the task you have been set. To do this, you need to understand what you are being asked to do by analysing the wording and meaning of the task instructions – **Step 5** in the 12-step process.

To understand the task, you need to break the instruction down into its component parts by asking yourself the following questions:

- **What's the *instruction?*** Many assignments are not questions but framed as commands introduced by an instruction word. It is important to interpret these instruction words properly (Table 8.2).

- **What's the *topic?*** This will clarify the context of the discussion you will need to construct.

- **What's the *aspect of the topic?*** This will help you define a more specific focus within the wider context and so define the relevant areas of research and reading.

- **What *restrictions* are imposed on the topic?** This will limit the scope of your research, reading and discussion.

Example assignment analysis

Task: 'Assess the importance of post-operative care in the rehabilitation of orthopaedic patients.'

Instruction: assess (= decide on the value or importance)

Topic: care (as in health care)

Aspect: importance (not the cost or any other aspect)

Restriction 1: post-operative (only post- not pre-operative care)

Restriction 2: rehabilitation (only the recovery phase and not the earlier phases)

Restriction 3: orthopaedic patients (only those and no other category)

Table 8.2 shows a range of typical instruction words, with definitions for each one. You should make sure you know what's expected of you when any of these instructions are used, not only in terms of these definitions but also in relation to the thinking processes expected (**Ch 11**). However, always take the whole task or question into account when deciding this.

Generally, instruction words in Table 8.2 fall into four categories, although this grouping may vary according to the context. The information box defines these instruction word categories in broad terms, and suggests differences in the approach you can take to tackling assignments that will dictate how you need to organise the information in your written submission.

Instruction word categories

One way of categorising instruction words is by looking at what they ask you to do:

Do – create something, draw up a plan, calculate

Describe – explain or show how something appears, happens or works

Analyse – look at all sides of an issue (there are often more than two)

Argue – look at all sides of an issue and provide supporting evidence for your view.

Table 8.2 Instruction words for assignments and exams. These words are the product of research into the frequency of use of the most common instruction words in university examinations. The definitions below are suggestions: you must take the whole question into account when answering.

Instruction word	Definition – what you are expected to do
Account [give an]	Describe
Account for	Give reasons for
Analyse	Give an organised answer looking at all aspects
Apply	Put a theory into operation
Assess	Decide on value/importance
Brief account [give a]	Describe in a concise way
Comment on	Give your opinion
Compare [with]	Discuss similarities; draw conclusions on common areas
Compile	Make up (a list/plan/outline)
Consider	Describe/give your views on the subject
Contrast	Discuss differences/draw own view
Criticise	Point out weak/strong points, i.e. give a balanced answer
Define	Give the meaning of a term, concisely
Demonstrate	Show by example/evidence
Describe	Provide a narrative on process/appearance/operation/sequence ...
Devise	Make up
Discuss	Give own thoughts and support your opinion or conclusion
Evaluate	Decide on merit of situation/argument
Exemplify	Show by giving examples
Expand	Give more information
Explain	Give reason for/say why
Explain how	Describe how something works
Identify	Pinpoint/list
Illustrate	Give examples
Indicate	Point out, but not in great detail
Justify	Support the argument for ...
List	Make an organised list, e.g. events, components, aspects
Outline	Describe basic factors/limited information
Plan	Think how to organise something
Report	Give an account of the process or event
Review	Write a report/give facts and views on facts
Show	Demonstrate with supporting evidence
Specify	Give details of something
State	Give a clear account of ...
Summarise	Briefly give an account
Trace	Provide a brief chronology of events/process
Work out	Find a solution, e.g. as in a maths problem

How should I respond to 'question words'?

Not all tasks are based on instructions; some do ask questions. For instance, they may include words such as 'How…?', 'Why…?' and expressions such as 'To what extent…?'. In these cases, you will need to think about what these mean within the do-describe-analyse-argue instruction hierarchy. One way to do this is to reword the question to assist your analysis of the task.

For example, consider the question: 'To what extent has the disposal of sewage effluence in rivers contributed to depletion of fish stocks over the last decade?'

This might be re-worded as: 'Outline the relationship between the disposal of sewage effluence in rivers and the depletion of fish stocks over the last decade'.

This would suggest a phased approach to organising the content of the answer to the original question (**Ch 15**).

You may already deconstruct questions, topics, assignments and other tasks subconsciously in this way, but there is value in marking these elements out on paper. First, it helps you to recognise the scope and limitations of the work you have been asked to complete. Second, it reduces the risk of producing a piece of work that waffles or strays from the point. Once you have gone through this quick process, you will be able to identify which resources or pieces of material are most suited to the task and so to your reading. Further discussion on the groups of instruction words follows in **Chapter 15**.

As you work through your reading and related note-making you will embark on **Step 6** of the 12-step process where you reflect more deeply on the topic. This will come about as you begin to be more discriminating about sources and the content they contain. As you move from basic texts to more specialised books or journal articles that give more detailed analysis, your understanding of the topic will expand. This may mean, for example, that you begin to build up, for example, a more informed picture of events, implications of a procedure or the possible solutions to a problem. What are you looking for? For instance, this could be facts, examples, theories, information to support a particular viewpoint (evidence) or counter-arguments to provide balance in your analysis of the topic. As you become more familiar with the issues, the easier it will be to think critically about what you are reading (**Ch 11**) and consequently build your response to the task you have been set.

PRACTICAL TIPS FOR ORGANISING YOURSELF FOR WRITING

Explore the full range of material available. In the early years of university study, many students follow the same practices as they used at school, often with too much reliance on handouts and/or notes from a single core textbook. At university you will be expected to read more widely by identifying source material beyond titles given as a basic starting point. You may benefit from exploring your library by browsing in areas related to your studies. There may be a whole range of material that has potential to expand your reading and understanding.

Spend an appropriate amount of time reading. This is a vital part of the writing process, but you should recognise the dangers of prolonging the reading phase beyond your scheduled deadline as noted previously. Students may delay moving on to the planning and writing steps because they are uncomfortable with writing. Facing up to these next steps and getting on with them is much less formidable once you get started, so it's best to stick to your time plan for this assignment and move on to the next step in the planned sequence.

Conserve material. In the process of marshalling information for a writing task, you will probably obtain some interesting and potentially useful material that proves to be irrelevant to the current writing task. Keeping this information may help at a later date for further assignments or exam revision. This personal cache of information could be useful in revitalising your knowledge and understanding of the topic.

 And now ...

8.1 Practise categorising instruction words. Go to Table 8.2 and mark out all those instructions that would invite a response asking you to do something practical, describe, analyse or construct an argument.

8.2 Examine some of the assignment titles that you will have to complete in a selected subject. Taking the whole question into account, identify what type of approach is needed – doing something practical, describing, analysing or arguing. You may find that within the same question/task you will have to do some describing in order to analyse or argue. The key is to avoid devoting too much time to the descriptive element at the expense of analysis/argument. You could also apply this activity when revising by using questions from past exam papers.

8.3 Try creating the wording for a task in a selected subject for yourself. Think about the clarity of the wording of your task. Is it ambiguous? Is it unclear? Identify your topic, aspect and restriction(s). Reversing the student-examiner roles can sometimes be a helpful way of developing your understanding. This could be an excellent preparation for exams because it helps with anticipating possible exam questions and reflecting on how you would answer them. This can help to broaden the range of possible questions you could feel comfortable tackling in exams.

THE FORMAT OF ACADEMIC WRITING

How to structure your text appropriately

Working towards your writing goals in an organised way is essential for success. In the initial stages, much time can be wasted through doubt, indecision, and lack of focus about what has to be achieved to get good grades for written assessments. This often arises because students are unaware of how to put together a piece of writing into a format that is acceptable for academic purposes. This chapter presents some fundamentals that will provide clarity about what you need to know about the contexts and practices of academic writing.

KEY TOPICS

→ General to specific to general format

→ Characteristics of introduction, main body and conclusion

→ Models of planning and writing introductions and conclusions

→ Taking word limits into account

KEY UNIVERSITY TERMS

Appendix/appendices   Bibliography   Citation

As we saw in **Chapters 1–7**, academic discussion tends to follow a relatively simple format comprising three main elements – introduction – main body – conclusion. It is on this basic framework that different types of academic assignment are constructed (**Ch 15**). Each section can be expanded or contracted to suit the task that you have been set, although the fundamental shape remains the same. You need to be conscious of this in the information-processing phase since this will help you with **Step 7** of the 12-step writing process in which you plan your writing (**Table 1.1**).

GENERAL TO SPECIFIC TO GENERAL FORMAT

The underpinning construction of academic writing follows the convention of moving from the general (the introduction) through to specific (the main body) and back to the general (the conclusion). Clearly, there has to be a balance over these three elements. Each situation will dictate the balance to some extent. In general, an introduction that is longer than the main body of the work or a conclusion of only a few lines will not be well received. Sometimes marks are allocated to each of the elements; therefore, a detailed introduction will not compensate for a weak main body nor a skimpy conclusion. Similarly, an introduction that is too brief and an overlong conclusion can be similarly detrimental to achieving a good mark.

In most subjects, in addition, you would be expected to provide a list of references (sometimes called 'bibliography' or 'work listed') which allows the reader to see the extent of your reading and, if they wish, the opportunity to consult some of the resources (**Ch 12**).

In some disciplines, you might include a glossary or word list that provides meanings of terms used in the specialist context. An appendix might also be included if there is additional material that might be useful to the reader but whose detail would interrupt the flow of the text were it included in the main body. Not all discipline conventions allow these additions; you can confirm whether these apply in your case by consulting your course handbook or subject area on your virtual learning environment.

CHARACTERISTICS OF INTRODUCTION, MAIN BODY AND CONCLUSION

The introduction, main body and conclusion perform distinctive functions in presenting your response to the task.

The introduction

At its most basic, this consists of three components:

1 a brief explanation of the context of the topic
2 an outline of the topic or issue as you understand it
3 an explanation of how you plan to address the topic in this particular paper – in effect, a statement of intent.

The introductory section may take several paragraphs to lay out these three dimensions. This should be done with some thought because this will indicate to your reader where you expect to take them in the main body of the text. In this way the introduction lays down the parameters that you have set yourself for this piece of work. For example, your topic may be multi-faceted and the word limit imposed on the work will not allow you to give a comprehensive coverage of all aspects. It is better to acknowledge the extensive nature of the topic and note that you are going to limit your discussion to only some of these aspects – usually those you consider to be most important or relevant to the topic. You need to explain the reasons for this decision at this stage.

The introduction as work in progress

This is the first contact that your reader makes with you as the author of the text. This means that the introduction has to be well organised and clear. However, to achieve this it is important to see the introductory section as 'work in progress' as your writing proceeds because, until you complete the entire text, you cannot really introduce the whole work accurately. Indeed, some people prefer to start writing the main body, move on to the conclusion and then write the introduction based on their draft text.

The main body

This section lays out your work based on the approach you decide to adopt in organising the content (**Ch 15**). You will have explained the approach in the introduction and this will mean that you should have mapped out your route for explaining your points.

In this section, you may need to generalise, describe, define or provide examples as part of your analysis. Here, it's important to keep the wording as concise, yet as clear, as possible. The construction of your paragraphs will be dictated by what you are trying to do at any particular point (different types of paragraph structures are outlined in **Table 16.3**).

Can I use sub-headings in my written work?

In some disciplines, sub-headings are acceptable, in others they are not. For most types of reports, sub-headings are expected. Where sub-headings are unacceptable, you may nevertheless find them useful to include in word-processed drafts as they can represent the structure of your writing plan. This will help to prevent you from digressing into irrelevant areas or presenting an apparently rambling paper. You can delete the sub-headings, or 'translate' them into topic sentences (**Ch 16**) to link paragraphs or introduce new themes.

The conclusion

This summarises the whole piece of work. You should review the entire text in three elements:

1 a restatement of the question and what you consider are the important features of the topic

2 a summary of the specific evidence that you have presented in support of your views

3 a statement of your overall viewpoint on the topic.

What mainly distinguishes the conclusion from the introduction is language. In the introduction, your explanation should be given clearly, avoiding specialist or technical words where possible. In the conclusion, you will be writing about the detail of the content and, therefore, the terminology you use is more likely to contain technical or more sophisticated language because you will have introduced this in the main body. You should avoid introducing new ideas in the conclusion that have not already been discussed in the earlier part of the writing.

Mini-conclusions

As you become immersed in the writing process, you will become very familiar with the material and conclusions you have drawn along the way. By the time you come to write the conclusion to the whole work, this in-depth awareness may become diluted. To avoid this, as you complete each section note down the main ideas you considered and your view about them. If you note these mini-conclusions on a separate piece of paper, then this will provide the substance for your final conclusion.

MODELS OF PLANNING AND WRITING INTRODUCTIONS AND CONCLUSIONS

Understanding how all these elements fit together can seem a little abstract. Thus, a practical sample plan is shown in Example 9.1. This follows the structure described in this chapter and is suggested as a model for writing for students new to university study. The level of detail is given to demonstrate the logic of the discussion. Each numbered sub-heading would be developed possibly as separate paragraphs. **Appendix 4** provides a further sample plan for a more advanced level of work. The topic could apply to more than one discipline, and this would affect the interpretation of the task and the content of the response.

Appendix 5 provides some sample introductions and conclusions explaining relative strengths and weaknesses. These relate to the topic and longer model answer in **Appendix 4**.

TAKING WORD LIMITS INTO ACCOUNT

Word limits are imposed, not to relieve tutors of marking, but to train you to be concise in your writing and to analyse the topic carefully to decide what to keep in and what to leave out.

Falling short of the word limit is just as bad as over-running the maximum. Some students keep a running total of words they have used and as soon as they reach the minimum word limit, they stop abruptly. This is not a good approach because it is more likely to leave a ragged and poorly considered piece of text that comes to an unexpected halt rather than one which is well planned, relevant and concisely written.

You should usually plan and write your first draft keeping only a casual eye on word count at this stage. When you come to editing that draft, you can prune and re-shape your writing. In this way it becomes a tighter piece of prose that falls within the maximum-minimum word limits imposed by the regulations and achieves a balance across the three elements.

Example 9.1 Model plan for response for an assignment on an undergraduate-style topic.

The detail given here is to demonstrate the technique. The reference list would follow the text and in line with the citation and referencing style you have been instructed to adopt (**Ch 12**).

Writing task:

Assess the use of the internet for the purpose of spreading information.

1. INTRODUCTION

1.1 Define the terms of reference for this writing assignment

    1.1.1 What is the internet? Explain its evolution and development to date

    1.1.2 What is meant by 'information'?

1.2 Define the parameters of the discussion by outlining the format of the text stating the limitations of the discussion and giving the reason for limitation.

    1.2.1 Identification of categories of user

    1.2.2 Recognition of positive aspects of internet

    1.2.3 Recognition of negative aspects of internet

    1.2.4 Acknowledgement of future potential

2. MAIN BODY

2.1 Categories of user

    2.1.1 Governmental/political

    2.1.2 Industrial users

    2.1.3 Commercial users

    2.1.4 Academic/research users

    2.1.5 General comment about diversity and egalitarianism

    2.1.6 Mini-conclusion

2.2 Positive aspects of internet

    2.2.1 Global nature of communication – ignore political/ideological/racial/ language limits

    2.2.2 Educational value

    2.2.3 Marketing value

    2.2.4 Public information e.g. health awareness

    2.2.5 Accessibility

    2.2.6 Mini-conclusion

2.3 Negative aspects of internet – divides into four subsets:

    2.3.1 Cost

    2.3.2 Reduction of personal interaction

    2.3.3 Security

    2.3.4 Potential for criminal abuse

    2.3.5 Mini-conclusion

2.4 Future potential of internet to disseminate information

    2.4.1 For good

    2.4.2 For bad

    2.4.3 Mini-conclusion

3. CONCLUSION

3.1 In the light of the case you have presented: What is your view on the subject? Based on:

    3.1.1 Mini-conclusion 1: categories of user

    3.1.2 Mini-conclusion 2: positive aspects

    3.1.3 Mini-conclusion 3: negative aspects

    3.1.4 Mini-conclusion 4: future potential

3.2 Your conclusion from the evidence presented:

    3.2.1 Is the internet an effective disseminator of information – yes or no?

    3.2.2 Are there/are there not alternative/better ways?

Should I limit the number of paragraphs in my assignment? ❓

The number of paragraphs required in an assignment is not usually defined in the UK although this is not always the case in some cultures. For example, essay-writing has a long history having evolved in different formats across continents and ages. Some formats were dictated by bureaucratic requirements as in the highly prescriptive classic style of the Chinese 'Eight-legged essay', while others have followed the traditions of ancient rhetoric offering an introduction followed by narration, confirmation, refutation and conclusion. More modern models follow for a five-paragraph format, recommended in some universities in the USA, for example. However, in the UK it would be unusual for students to be asked to confine themselves to a fixed number of paragraphs. The UK system tends to follow a simpler model comprising three elements – introduction, main body and conclusion. Each element has the potential to be constructed using the number of paragraphs that you, as the writer, consider necessary to cover the points you wish to make while keeping within the prescribed word limit. This can be done following the patterns suggested in **Chapter 15** and modelled in Example 9.1.

Counting words

Most word processors include a word-count function that can be used either for entire documents or for selected text. Microsoft Word also incorporates features that allow you to keep a running word total, either in the status bar or as a floating toolbar. The exact details of how to enable these features depend on the program version, so if you wish to use them, consult the 'help' feature or search for online tutorials.

PRACTICAL TIPS FOR FOLLOWING CLASSIC FORMATS IN YOUR ACADEMIC WRITING

Keep the right proportions in your response. Make sure that the three elements within your writing framework are well balanced in extent. The main body should be the most substantial piece of the writing, whereas the introduction and conclusion should occupy much less space. A common problem for many new students is that they devote too much time to outlining the context in the introduction and leave themselves with too little time and space to get to the core of the discussion in the paper.

Once you have completed your draft, review the introduction. Go back to the introduction. Make sure that you have actually done what you set out to do when defining the parameters of your work and in your statement of intent. The act of writing your text may have stimulated new thoughts, and your initial intentions may have altered in the process of writing.

Pay adequate attention to the conclusion. By the time that students reach the conclusion, writing it is often done at some speed because there may be other demands on their time, or the initial interest in the subject may have palled, or they may simply be tired. Thus, conclusions often don't get the attention they deserve. You should reserve some time to give your conclusion a critical appraisal and even consider writing this section before finishing the perhaps more 'mechanical' earlier parts. Alternatively, you could 'write it as you go' by keeping detailed notes of key points separately as mini-conclusions that you can use to frame your conclusion once you have written the main body.

Support your work with appropriate citations and a reference list. In most, if not all, disciplines, you will be expected to include reference to recognised authorities within the field you are studying. This helps to validate the ideas and concepts you are discussing. For example, in law, this could be cases; in the arts and humanities, work of a renowned academic; in the sciences, research that establishes the precedence of findings and ideas. This does not mean that you need to quote substantial pieces of text; you can summarise the idea in your own words and then follow the rules about citation that are given in **Chapter 12**. All of this needs to be taken into consideration in planning and drafting your writing within the basic structural framework.

Think about appendices. Sometimes the length of your text may be seriously beyond the word limit. This means that some drastic 'surgery' is required. One approach might be to remove some parts of the text and, while remaining within the word limit, reduce the information contained to bullet-point lists. The detail can then be placed in an appendix or appendices, making appropriate cross-references in the main text. Clearly, this is a strategy that has to be used sparingly, but it can be helpful in some situations, if allowed. Look to your course handbook to confirm this point because some departments may consider appendices to be part of the text for word-counting purposes.

 And now ...

9.1 Compare textual patterns. Go back to a textbook for your subject, select a chapter and identify the proportion of space allocated to introducing the entire chapter. How much is reserved for the conclusion? Recognising the balance that professional writers achieve in their text may be helpful when you frame your own writing.

9.2 Track the pattern of your writing. Go back to an existing piece of your own writing and try to identify that you have the basic elements and sub-elements of the standard writing format in place. Are the introduction, main body and conclusion identifiable? Does the introduction contain the elements of context, specific focus and statement of intent? For the conclusion, is your position laid out clearly and with supporting rationale? If any of your answers are negative, try to work out how you could improve things.

9.3 Practise converting sub-headings to topic sentences. Take a piece of your own writing or a section from a textbook where sub-headings have been used. Try to create a topic sentence (**Ch 5** and **Ch 16**) that could replace that sub-heading. Decide which is more effective in this instance – the topic sentence or the original sub-heading. Consider why this is the case. Again, this should be instructive in processing information and shaping the style you adopt in your own writing.

10

FOLLOWING THE EXPECTED ACADEMIC STYLE IN YOUR WRITING

How to adopt the appropriate language conventions in your task

The stylistic codes you need to follow in academic writing are rarely comprehensively defined. This chapter will help you understand what it means to write in an academic style and outlines some forms of language to avoid and some to follow.

KEY TOPICS

→ What is academic style?

→ Being objective

→ Appropriate use of tense

→ Appropriate use of vocabulary

→ Non-academic versus academic language

KEY UNIVERSITY TERMS

Acronym   Colloquial   Idiom   Noun   Phrasal verb
Pronoun   Register   Rhetorical question   Verb

University assignments can take several forms, such as an essay, a report, a project portfolio, a case study or a dissertation. One thing that is common to all these types of writing is that they need to follow academic style. This begins in **Step 8** in the 12-step writing process, that is, in creating your first draft. While it is possible to identify differences between 'scientific' and 'humanities' styles in the finer detail, this chapter covers the common features of all types of academic writing.

WHAT IS ACADEMIC STYLE?

Academic style involves the use of precise and objective language to express ideas. It must be grammatically correct, and is more formal than the style used in novels, newspapers, informal correspondence and everyday conversation. This should mean that the language is clear and simple. It does not imply that it is complex, pompous and dry. Above all, academic style is *objective*, using language techniques that generally maintain an impersonal tone and a vocabulary that is more succinct, rather than involving personal, colloquial, or idiomatic expressions.

 Why is less formal writing not better?

There are various reasons for using more formal language or 'register' in academic writing. For example:

■ informal language is, by its very nature, limited and imprecise

■ informal language is closely related to speech and, for this reason, it may be perceived as emotive and less objective in style

■ informal writing may appear to be a less than serious attempt to respond to the task.

BEING OBJECTIVE

When writing academically, it is important that your personal involvement with your topic does not overshadow the importance of what you are commenting on or reporting. The main way of demonstrating this lack of bias is by using impersonal language. This means:

● avoiding personal pronouns – try not to use the following words:

I/me/one

you (singular and plural)

we/us

● using the passive rather than active voice – try to write about the action and not about the actor (the person who performed the action – see next page).

You can use other strategies to maintain an impersonal style in your writing. For general statements, you could use a structure such as 'It is ...', 'There is ...' or 'There are ...' to introduce sentences. For more specific points relating to statements you have already made, you could use the structures 'This is ...' or 'These are ...'. with appropriate tense changes according to the context. Don't forget that when you use words like 'it', 'this', or 'these', there should be no ambiguity over the word or phrase to which they refer. Clarity can be achieved by introducing a defining word (noun), for example, 'this explanation ...' or 'these results ...'

Another way in which you can maintain objectivity by writing impersonally is to change the verb in the sentence to a noun and then reframe the sentence in a less personal way.

We **applied** pressure to the wound to stem bleeding (*verb in bold*).
becomes
The **application** of pressure stemmed bleeding (*noun in bold*).

This kind of text-juggling will become second nature as you tackle more and more assignments.

Passive and active voice

This is best explained from examples:

- Pressure **was applied** to the wound to stem bleeding (passive).
- We **applied** pressure to the wound to stem bleeding (active).

Some would argue that the second example is clearer, but their opponents would counter-argue that the use of 'we' takes attention away from the action.

You may find that the grammar checkers in some word-processing packages suggest that passive expressions should be changed to active. However, if you follow this guidance, you will find yourself having to use a personal pronoun, which is inconsistent with impersonal academic style. If in doubt, ask your tutors for their preference.

APPROPRIATE USE OF TENSE

The past tense is used in academic writing to describe or comment on things that have already happened. However, there are times when the present tense is appropriate. For example, in a report you might write 'Figure 5 shows …' (because it continues to show), rather than 'Figure 5 showed …', when describing your results. A material and methods section, on the other hand, will always be in the past tense, because it describes what you *did*.

In colloquial English, there is often a tendency to misuse tenses. This can creep into academic assignments, especially where the author is narrating a sequence of events.

The following examples illustrate two ways of writing a paragraph using different tenses:

> Napoleon **orders** his troops to advance on Moscow. The severe winter **closes** in on them and they **come back** a ragbag of an army. (Present tense in bold.)

and:

> Napoleon **ordered** his troops to advance on Moscow. The severe winter **closed** in on them and they **came back** a ragbag of an army. (Simple past tense in bold.)

While the first of these examples might work with the soundtrack of a documentary on Napoleon's Russian campaign, it is too colloquial for academic written formats.

Plain English

There has been a growing movement in recent times that advocates the use of 'plain English', and it has been very successful in persuading government departments and large commercial organisations to simplify written material for public reference. This has been achieved by introducing a less formal style of language that uses simpler, more active sentence structures, and a simpler range of vocabulary avoiding jargon. This is an admirable development. However, academic writing style needs to be precise, professional and unambiguous, and the strategies of 'plain English' campaigners may not be entirely appropriate to the style expected of you as an academic author. For the same reasons, some of the suggestions offered by software packages may be inappropriate to your subject and academic conventions.

APPROPRIATE USE OF VOCABULARY

Good academic writers think carefully about their choice of words. The 'plain English' movement (see previous page) recommends that words of Latin origin should be replaced by their Anglo-Saxon, or spoken, alternatives. However, this does not always contribute to the style and precision appropriate to academic authorship. For example, compare:

If we **turn down** the volume, then there will be no feedback.

and

If we **turn down** the offer from the World Bank, then interest rates will rise.

Both sentences are meaningful, but they use the two-word verb 'turn down' in different senses. These verbs are properly called phrasal verbs and they often have more than a single meaning. Furthermore, they are also used more in speech than in formal writing. Therefore, it would be better to write:

If we **reduce** the volume, then there will be no feedback.

and

If we **reject** the offer from the World Bank, then interest rates will rise.

The use of the Latin origin words 'reduce' and 'reject' ensures that the respective meanings are clear, concise and unambiguous. If you are restricted to a word limit on your work, using the one-word verb has additional obvious advantages. **Table 12.2** gives you the chance to explore some further two-word verbs and their one-word equivalents. **Chapter 15** explores other areas of vocabulary usage and development.

Non-sexist language

The Council of Europe recommends that, where possible, gender-specific language is avoided. Thus: 'S/he will provide specimens for her/his exam'. This is rather clumsy, but, by transforming the sentence into the plural, this is avoided: 'They will provide specimens for their exams'. Alternatively, if appropriate, 'you/your' could be used.

TRANSFORMING NON-ACADEMIC TO ACADEMIC LANGUAGE

You should think about the style of your writing when you review your written work (**Ch 17**). Table 10.1 gives a specific example of text conversion from informal to formal style. Table 10.2 provides several pointers to help you achieve a more academic style.

The common errors of language use to avoid in your writing are:

- poor grammar and imprecise wording (**Appendices 9** and **10**);
- use of personal pronouns (**Appendices 9** and **10**);
- colloquial language, such as idiom, slang and cliché (Table 10.2);
- absolute terms, when inappropriate (Table 10.2);
- value judgements (**Ch 11**); and
- easily rectified spelling and punctuation errors (**Appendices 7** and **8**).

Table 10.1 Example of converting a piece of 'non-academic' writing into academic style. Note that the conversion results in a slightly longer piece of text (47 versus 37 words). This emphasises the point that while you should aim for concise writing, precise wording may be more important.

Original text (non-academic style)	'Corrected' text (academic style)
In this country, we have changed the law so that the King or Queen is less powerful since the Great War. But he or she can still advise, encourage or warn the Prime Minister if they want.	In the United Kingdom, legislation has been a factor in the decline of the role of the monarchy in the period since the Great War. Nevertheless, the monarchy has survived and, thus, the monarch continues to exercise the right to advise, encourage and warn the Prime Minister.
Points needing correction	**Corrected points**
• Non-specific wording (*this country*)	• Specific wording (country specified: *in the United Kingdom*)
• Personal pronoun (*we*)	• Impersonal language (*legislation has*)
• Weak grammar (*but* is a connecting word and should not be used to start a sentence).	• Appropriate signpost word (*nevertheless*)
• Word with several meanings (*law*)	• Generic, yet well-defined term (*legislation*)
• Duplication of nouns (*king or queen*)	• Singular abstract term (*monarchy*)
• Inconsistent and potentially misleading pronoun use (*he or she, they*)	• Repeated subject (*monarch*) and reconstructed sentence
• Informal style (*can still*)	• More formal style (*continues to exercise*)

Table 10.2 Fundamentals of academic writing. These elements of academic writing are in alphabetical order. Being aware of these and training yourself to follow them will help you to develop as an academic author ensuring that you don't lose marks by making basic errors of usage or expression.

Abbreviations and acronyms
It is acceptable to use abbreviations in academic writing to express units, for example, SI units. Otherwise, abbreviations are generally reserved for note-taking. Thus, avoid: e.g. (for example), i.e. (that is), viz. (namely) in formal work.
Acronyms are a kind of abbreviation formed by taking the initial letters of a name of an organisation, a procedure or an apparatus, and then using these letters instead of writing out the title in full. Thus, World Health Organisation becomes WHO. The academic convention is that the first time that you use a title with an acronym alternative, then you should write it in full with the acronym in brackets immediately after the full title. Thereafter, within that document you can use the acronym. For example:
The European Free Trade Association (EFTA) has close links with the European Community (EC). Both EFTA and the EC require new members to have membership of the Council of Europe as a prerequisite for admission to their organisations.
In some forms of academic writing, for example formal reports, you may be expected to include a list of abbreviations in addition to these first-time-of-use explanations.

'Absolute' terms
In academic writing, it is important to be cautious about using absolute terms such as:
always and **never**; **most** and **all**; **least** and **none**.
This does not prevent you from using these words; it simply means that they should be used with caution, that is, when you are absolutely certain of your ground.

Clichés
Living languages change and develop over time. This means that some expressions come into such frequent usage that they lose their meaning; indeed, they can often be replaced with a much less long-winded expression. For example:
First and foremost (first); **last but not least** (finally); **at this point in time** (now).
This procedure is the **gold standard** of hip replacement methods.   (This procedure is the best hip replacement method.)
In the second example, 'gold standard' is completely inappropriate; correctly used, it should refer to monetary units, but it has been misused by being introduced into other contexts.

Table **10.2** continued

Colloquial language
This term encompasses informal language that is common in speech. Colloquialisms and idiomatic language should not be used in academic writing. This example shows how colloquial language involving cliché and idiom has been misused: **Not to beat about the bush**, increasing income tax did the Chancellor **no good at the end of the day** and he **was ditched** at the next Cabinet reshuffle. (Increasing income tax did not help the Chancellor and he was replaced at the next Cabinet reshuffle.)

'Hedging' language
For academic purposes, it is often impossible to state categorically that something is or is not the case. There are verbs that allow you to 'hedge your bets' by not coming down on one side or another of an argument, or which allow you to present a variety of different scenarios without committing yourself to any single position. **seems that   looks as if   suggests that   appears that.** This involves using a language construction that leaves the reader with the sense that the evidence presented is simply supporting a hypothetical, or imaginary, case. To emphasise this sense of 'hedging', the use of a special kind of verb is introduced. These modal verbs are: **can/cannot   could/could not   may/may not   might/might not.** These can be used with a variety of other verbs to increase the sense of tentativeness. For example: These results **suggest** that there has been a decline in herring stocks in the North Sea. Even more tentatively, this could be: These results **could suggest** that there has been a decline in herring stocks in the North Sea.

Jargon and specialist terms
Most subjects make use of language in a way that is exclusive to that discipline. It is important, therefore, to explain terms that a general reader might not understand. It is always good practice to define specialist terms or 'regular' words that are being used in a very specific way.

Rhetorical questions
Some writers use direct rhetorical questions as a stylistic vehicle to introduce the topic addressed by the question. This is a good strategy if you are making a speech and it can have some power in academic writing, although it should be used sparingly. Example: **How do plants survive in dry weather?** a rhetorical question, could be rephrased as: **Understanding how plants survive in dry weather is important.**

Split infinitives

One of the most commonly quoted split infinitives comes from the TV series *Star Trek* where Captain James T. Kirk states that the aim of the Star Ship Enterprise is 'to boldly go where no man has gone before'. This means that an adverb (boldly) has split the infinitive (to go). It should read as 'to go boldly'. Many traditionalists consider that the split infinitive is poor English, although modern usage increasingly ignores the rule. Nevertheless, it is probably better to avoid the split infinitive in academic writing, which tends to be particularly traditional.

Value judgements

These are defined as statements in which the author or speaker is providing an interpretation based on a subjective viewpoint (**Ch 11**). For example, a writer who states that 'Louis XIV was a rabid nationalist' without giving supporting evidence for this statement is not making an objective comment in a professional manner. Rewording this statement to: 'Louis XIV was regarded as a rabid nationalist. This is evident in the nature of his foreign policy where he ...' offers the reader some evidence that explains the claim.

 PRACTICAL TIPS FOR ENSURING THAT YOU WRITE IN AN ACADEMIC STYLE

Think about your audience. Your readers should direct the style you adopt for any writing you do. For example, if you were writing to your bank manager asking for a loan, you would not use text-messaging or informal language. Similarly, for academic writing, you should take into account that your reader(s) will probably be marking your work and, in addition to knowledge and content, they will be looking for evidence of awareness and correct use of specialist terms and structures.

Avoid contractions. In spoken English, shortened forms such as, *don't*, *can't*, *isn't*, *it's*, *I'd* and *we'll* are used all the time. However, in academic written English, they should not be used. Texting contractions are also inappropriate.

Avoid personal pronouns. Experiment with other language structures so that you avoid the personal pronouns, *I/me/one*, *you* and *we/us*, and their possessive forms, *my*, *your* and *our*.

GO And now ...

10.1 Take steps to improve your writing style. Correct English is essential in academic writing. **Appendices 9** and **10** present points about grammar that may apply to your work. Look at **Appendices 9** and **10** in order to understand the grammatical terms. Highlight points that you do not know at present and resolve to use this information in your written work. You may be able to find errors that your lecturers have identified in feedback on your work. Next, consult a grammar book (**Reference list**) to find out more about the relevant grammar point. You can consolidate your understanding by doing the exercises provided in such books.

10.2 Ask a friend to work with you on your writing style. Swap a piece of writing and check over your friend's writing and ask them to do the same for yours. When you have done this, compare the points you have found. Try to explain what you think could be improved. Together, you may be able to clarify some aspects that you were unaware were problematic. Afterwards look at **Appendix 9** and follow the suggestion in point 10.1 above.

10.3 Learn from published academic writing in your discipline. Look at a textbook or journal article – especially in the area that discusses results or evidence or recommendations. Try to find examples of the use of 'hedging' language (Table 10.2) and note what else authors do with language in order to ensure that they avoid making absolute judgements.

11

INFORMATION-PROCESSING AND CRITICAL THINKING FOR WRITING

How to approach your analysis of source material

Having collated information and viewpoints in preparation for writing, you need to identify and group ideas and evidence in support. You will need to filter out irrelevant, out-dated or inaccurate material. This information-processing will allow you to produce writing that explains your ideas clearly. This chapter guides you through this process.

KEY TOPICS

→ The types of information you may have to process

→ Thinking about thinking

→ Using method to organise your thoughts

→ Recognising fallacy and bias

→ Avoiding shallow thinking in your writing

KEY UNIVERSITY TERMS

Concept   Conjecture   Evidence   Fact   Fallacy
Hypothesis (pl. hypotheses)   Knowledge   Objectivity
Paradigm   Synonym   Subjectivity   Taxonomy   Theory

This chapter continues with **Step 8** of the 12-step writing process (**Ch 1**) by suggesting strategies of logic and interpretation that will assist you in processing information and opinion as you create your first draft. These strategies will encourage you to engage in critical thinking and so to discriminate between facts, concepts, theories, hypotheses and evidence.

As with many tasks, the key to good writing is in the preparation and, as noted in **Chapters 1** to **7**, the information gathering phase is part of that preparation. The lecture notes, the notes from recommended and supplementary reading, ideas noted from tutorial discussion and your own thoughts contribute to the mix, as does your willingness to approach university study with an open mind that is receptive to analysing new ideas or challenging older ones. In assembling this information, you will already have engaged in some aspect of critical thinking by making a judgement about what to include and what to exclude.

 Definition: critical

People often interpret the words 'critical' and 'criticism' to mean being negative about an issue. For university work, the alternative meaning of 'making a careful judgement after balanced consideration of all aspects of a topic' is one that you should adopt.

THE TYPES OF INFORMATION YOU MAY HAVE TO PROCESS

To understand what it means to think critically, you will need to be aware of the significance of different types of information. Some examples are shown in Table 11.1, namely, concepts, evidence, facts, hypotheses, ideas, knowledge, paradigms and theory. These terms are part of the language of the academic world. Therefore, gaining a full understanding of their meaning as applied to academic discussion is a vital part of your development as an academic writer. Table 11.1 provides a meaning applicable to the use of these terms in the academic community (Chambers Dictionary, 2003), since less formal usage may be less precise. Lecturers often use certain terms interchangeably, therefore, synonyms for each term are given in the third column so that you are aware of words similar in meaning that might be used as an alternative form of expression.

Sometimes students are confused by what someone presents as information when it is simply unsupported opinion or guesswork. Consequently, when evaluating information, you need to recognise the importance of differentiating the nature of information you encounter.

Thus, while some pieces of information represent facts, knowledge relates to a more refined set of structured facts; those that are the nearest to reality. In the academic sense, theory and hypothesis are

Table 11.1 **Terms used in academic discussion**

Term	Explanation	Synonyms
Concept	Abstract idea, mental impression, general notion, any product of intellectual action, of memory or imagination	• Conception • Notion • Opinion • Thought • Viewpoint
Evidence	Available body of facts or information indicating whether a belief or proposition is true; means of proving an unknown or disputed fact; support for a belief	• Proof • Testimony
Fact	A thing that is indisputably the case, a reality (as distinct from a statement or a belief)	• Actuality • Case • Circumstance • Deed • Reality • Truth
Hypothesis	(Sciences) An explanation of reality that is testable by observation or experiment. (Non-sciences) A proposition assumed for the sake of argument	• Assumption • Conjecture • Premise • Presumption • Supposition
Idea	An image of an external object formed by the mind; a notion, thought or impression, any product of intellectual action, of memory or imagination	• Design • Proposal • Thought
Knowledge	What is known in a particular field; an assured belief	• Cognition • Enlightenment • Information • Science
Paradigm	A particularly well-established theory or set of theories, one that governs understanding and practice across an entire field of study	• Concept • Scientific consensus • Theoretical framework
Theory	A supposition or system of ideas intended to explain something that is based on evidence, but which nevertheless may change if new evidence or understanding comes to light; a set of principles on which a practice or activity is based	• Assumption • Proposition • Thesis

testable notions of reality that are supported by existing knowledge, but that can be refined or rejected as a result of further observation or experiment. Concepts and viewpoints reflect the ideas of individuals groups and arise from intellectual processing. They may reflect opinion that may have little or no foundation in terms of truth, evidence or accuracy. In summary, depending on contexts, these terms can reflect certainty or uncertainty. Recognising these distinctions will help you to reach an understanding of the thinking processes that apply when you process information.

Exercise healthy scepticism

Just because information or views have been published within the covers of a book or an article appears on the internet or has been written by an apparently eminent authority, this does not mean that the content is based on fact or even valid. Be more challenging when reading by looking at flaws in an argument, data that are not accurately presented or viewpoints that are biased. Similarly, be aware of material that may come from unconfirmed sources, such as a blog or personal website. Come to your own conclusions based on your own research, knowledge and understanding of the topic area.

THINKING ABOUT THINKING

Novice writers have to make quite sophisticated selections from different information types, and so knowing how and where these might be used in constructing text will be helpful. A useful model to explain this is a taxonomy or classification created by researchers led by Benjamin Bloom. This identifies six key learning objectives typically involved in processing thought and is outlined in Table 11.2.

Bloom *et al.* (1956) showed that students naturally engaged in thought-processing during their studies. For example, from Table 11.2, you may recognise that your school work mainly focussed on knowledge, comprehension and application. These levels of thinking can lead to heavily descriptive or narrative writing that will earn few marks in higher education, if overdone. By contrast, your university tutors tend to expect more evidence of analysis, synthesis and evaluation, namely, the 'higher order' skills of information- and thought-processing.

These expectations are sometimes closely linked to the instruction words used in assessments and Column 3 of Table 11.2 provides a few examples. Thus when you analyse the instructions used in writing assignments, you should take into account what type of thinking process the examiner has asked you to carry out, and try your best to reach the required level. However, take care when interpreting these instruction words, as processes and tasks may mean different things in different subjects. For example, while 'describe' might imply a 'lower order' activity in the sciences, it might involve 'higher order' skills in subjects like architecture.

Certain disciplines value 'creativity' as a thinking process, for example, Art and Design, Architecture, Drama or English. Creativity involves notions of novelty and originality associated with invention, imagination and/or problem solving. In some cases, this term might take the place of 'synthesis' in Table 11.2, whilst in others, it would even be ranked above 'evaluation'. You may also come across the terms 'originality' or 'original work' in learning objectives and marking scales, indicating an expectation for this type of creativity in your university work.

Consequently, the success with which you apply the instruction words in your writing, as these apply to your discipline, shows markers that you are attuned to the more exacting demands of higher education. This will be reflected in higher grades for your written work.

Contexts for thinking critically

Examples of university work involving high level thinking skills include:

■ Essay writing in the arts and social sciences

■ Reports on problem-based learning in medicine and nursing

■ Case-based scenarios in law

■ Reports on project-based practical work in the sciences

Table 11.2 Classification of thinking processes (Bloom *et al.* 1956). The learning objectives shown in Column 1 comprise a classification commonly referred to as 'Bloom's Taxonomy'. Some refinement of the Taxonomy has been conducted by more recent researchers and their preferred use of 'action verbs' rather than nouns to explain the classification is reflected in Column 2 (relevant verbs italicised). The representative examples also shown Column 2 might apply to academic work in an Arts subject such as History or Politics. Column 3 illustrates the types of question/instruction verbs used by tutors when they construct assignment and exam 'questions' and that they use to imply that relevant thought processes are required on the part of the student.

Learning objectives (in perceived ascending order of difficulty)	Requirement for expressing thinking at each level followed by an example of such thinking in academic use.	Representative verbs (e.g. 'instruction words' in tasks)
1. Knowledge	**The ability *to remember* previously learned information.** For example, a student might know that a particular river was an important boundary in terms of international relations, but without being able to identify why.	• Define • Describe • Identify • Order • Outline • State
2. Comprehension	**The ability *to demonstrate* an understanding of the facts.** For example, a student might understand that the river forms a natural barrier which can easily be identified and defended.	• Classify • Discuss • Identify • Paraphrase • Review • Summarise
3. Application	**The ability *to apply* knowledge to actual situations.** For example, a student might use their knowledge and comprehension to explain the terms of a peace treaty that refers to the river as a boundary.	• Demonstrate • Illustrate • Manipulate • Modify • Predict • Solve
4. Analysis	**The ability *to break down* objects or ideas into simpler parts and find evidence to support *generalisation*.** For example, a student might explain the importance of river boundary as being of importance to the territorial gains/losses for the signatories to the peace treaty.	• Appraise • Calculate • Compare • Contrast • Explain • Question

Table 11.2 continued

Learning objectives (in perceived ascending order of difficulty)	Requirement for expressing thinking at each level followed by an example of such thinking in academic use.	Representative verbs (e.g. 'instruction words' in tasks)
5. Synthesis	**The ability *to compile* component ideas into a new whole or propose alternative solutions.** For example, a student might identify the concept of 'rivers as geopolitical boundaries' and its recurrence in later or analogous treaties and explain how this had governed accompanying hostilities and associated negotiations.	• Arrange • Compose • Create • Develop • Reorganize • Summarize
6. Evaluation	**The ability *to make* and *defend* judgements based on internal evidence or external criteria, thus implying creativity.** For example, a student might form a judgement as to whether the use of this boundary was an obstacle to resolving the treaty to satisfy all parties.	• Argue • Assess • Draw a conclusion • Judge • Recommend • Support

USING METHOD TO PROMPT AND ORGANISE YOUR THOUGHTS

In written work, a degree of description will often be required to demonstrate knowledge, comprehension and application (Bloom's Taxonomy – Table 11.2). Such descriptions might be confined to explaining a context by simply presenting facts, but in academic work, this description could also involve outlining concepts, hypotheses or theories to establish a context for the main body of the writing.

Many new students do not realise that, although perhaps acceptable at school, description alone is insufficient for an essay at university level of study. Consequently, they lose marks in their writing because they simply restate facts or statements, that is, without explaining their importance and context, or without showing their understanding of what the material means or implies. Such writing would probably be regarded as superficial narrative that does not demonstrate a student's ability to process complex information.

To move forward, students need to develop ways of processing the information to create writing that meets the university standard. This relies on critical thinking to reach a logical conclusion and involves steps such as those listed below. You should regard this listing as a menu rather than a recipe – think about the different elements and how they might be useful for the specific issue under consideration and your own style of work. Adopt or reject them, or chop and change the order in which you use them as you see fit.

- **Go back to basic information.** Revisit the learning outcomes for your module or course. Work out how these relate to your topic and the writing required (**Step 1** in the 12-step process of writing).

- **Make sure you fully grasp the nature of the task.** This relates to **Steps 5–8** in the 12-step writing process. Thus, if a specific question has been given as part of the exercise, then analyse its phrasing carefully to make sure you understand all possible meanings (**Table 8.2**). When analysing the instructions used in writing assignments, you should take into account the type of thinking process the examiner has asked you to carry out, and try your best to reach the required level (Table 11.2). If you have been given a general topic, rather than a detailed question or instruction, then write down a brief description of the aspects you wish to address to clarify the terminology and concepts involved.

- **Review and check the information you have collected.** You need to ensure that you fully understand what you have gathered. This could be as simple as using dictionaries and specialist reference sources to find out the precise meaning of key words. Cross-checking explanations in different sources can also help.

- **Organise your approach to the task in three phases.**

    1 **Open thinking**. Consider the issue or question from all possible angles or positions and write down everything that comes to mind. Don't worry at this stage about the relevance or importance of your ideas. You may wish to use a 'spider diagram' or 'mind map' to lay out your thoughts (**Figure A2.5**).

    2 **Analysis.** Now you need to decide about the relevance of the grouped points to the original problem. Typical groupings include:
       - classifications
       - time-sequenced events
       - support and opposition/counterargument for a viewpoint
       - comparison or contrast of issues or perspectives
       - cause and effect relationships

Reject trivial or irrelevant ideas and rank or prioritise those that seem relevant. A new diagram, table or grid may make things clearer.

3 **Synthesis and evaluation.** Think through your argument, and work out how you can support it. Having considered relevant information and positions, you should arrive at a personal approach or viewpoint, and then construct your discussion or conclusion around this. When writing about your conclusion, you must take care to avoid value judgments or other kinds of expression of opinion that are not supported by evidence or sources. This is one reason why frequent citation and referencing are demanded in academic work.

What are value judgements?

A value judgement is a statement based primarily on a subjective viewpoint of opinion rather than an objective analysis of facts. It is therefore influenced by the 'value system' of the writer or the speaker. Value systems involve such matters as ethics, morals, behavioural norms and religious standpoints that are embedded from a person's upbringing and hence influence their views on external matters, sometimes unwittingly. A value judgement may be detected through the use of 'loaded' language (consider, for example, potentially contrasting usage of 'freedom fighter', 'insurgent' and 'guerrilla'. One aim of academic analysis is to minimise subjectivity of this type by evaluating all aspects of an issue and focussing on logical interpretation of facts.

RECOGNISING FALLACY AND BIAS

A logical approach is essential for academic arguments and discussions. As a writer, you must develop the ability to analyse the logic of others' viewpoints and you must ensure that your own text follows a clear logical path. To do this, you need to detach yourself from the argument itself and think about the way in which it is conducted. One of the best ways of developing this skill this is to study the ways in which logic and argument break down through fallacy and bias. There are many different types of logical fallacies. A few common examples are listed in **Appendix 3** to show you the sorts of things that may arise.

Definitions

Bias – information that emphasises just one viewpoint or position

Fallacy – a fault in logic or thinking that means that an argument is incorrect

Propaganda – false or incomplete information that supports a particular political or moral view.

Once tuned in to this way of thinking, you should be able to observe that faulty logic and debating tricks are frequently used in areas such as advertising and politics. Analysing the methods being used can be a useful way of practising your critical skills.

Bias is the use of selected information to support a viewpoint. One way of avoiding bias in your own work is to try to balance your discussion by considering different viewpoints rather than just confining your writing to presenting a single viewpoint. Furthermore, students frequently assume that there are two opposing positions on an issue, when in fact there could be multiple views. You should acknowledge these in your text, even though you might confine your in-depth discussion to the more well-known, dominant or contrasting aspects.

In academic work it is important to recognise that knowledge and understanding may change through time. Hence, avoid 'absolutes' – be especially careful with words that imply that there are no exceptions, for example: 'always', 'never', 'all' and 'every'. These words can only be used if you are sure of facts that imply one hundred per cent certainty. **Table 10.2** provides further information on 'absolutes' and associated 'hedging' language.

Objectivity in your writing

If you want to communicate clearly in writing assignments, then it is important to adopt a style of writing that conveys your ideas in a way that presents an objective perspective on the topic (**Ch 10**). If you provide your reader with subjectively worded commentary, then they will be less likely to consider your work as a professional piece of writing. It is possible to write in a detached way, yet convey that the views are personal.

AVOIDING SHALLOW THINKING IN YOUR WRITING

Aside from fallacy, bias and plain and simple error, there are many other ways in which students' thinking may be faulty or shallow. Typical examples include:

- generalising
- thinking in terms of stereotypes
- personalising
- over-simplifying
- using arguments based on incorrect assumptions
- using outdated information as evidence
- making value judgements
- making unsupported statements using absolute terms
- rushing to conclusions.

To avoid these sorts of faults in your own writing, engage in critical thinking, so that you:

- base your points on information that is specific
- appraise viewpoints that have been well-debated
- explain complex content clearly and fairly
- reach conclusions based on measured consideration of all aspects of evidence.

 PRACTICAL TIPS FOR CRITICAL THINKING AND INFORMATION PROCESSING IN WRITING

Keep an open mind when you approach a new assignment. Although you may start with preconceived ideas about a topic, you should try to be receptive to the ideas of others. You may find that your initial thoughts have become altered by what you are reading and discussing. If there is not enough evidence to support any conclusion, be prepared to suspend judgement.

Draw on the ideas and opinions of your peers and tutors. Discussion with others can be very fruitful, revealing a range of interpretations that you might not have thought about yourself. You may find it useful to 'bounce ideas off' others in your group. Tutors can provide useful insights especially when you are participating in group activities such as tutorials or labs. This helps you to appreciate wider perspectives than those you first formed on your own.

Look beneath the surface. Decide whether sources are dealing with facts or opinions; examine any assumptions made, including your own; think about the motivation of writers. Rather than restating and describing your sources, focus on what they mean when they write.

(GO) And now ...

11.1 Scrutinize the depth of thinking in your own work. Select a past essay or assignment, then reflect on the thinking processes shown in Table 11.1 and identify the extent to which these are evident in your own writing. For example, the early sections may contain descriptive material or cite applications of a concept. Later parts may include deeper analysis and evaluation. If you are appropriately self-critical (itself an important thinking skill), you may recognise that you could perhaps have achieved a better balance between the 'lower order' and the later 'higher order' elements. This might connect with tutors' feedback on your work (Ch 18) and reveal how you could improve your marks.

11.2 Watch how different journalists present information to listeners, viewers and readers. Radio, television and newspaper reporters pass on information sometimes objectively and sometimes subjectively. Follow a single 'story' over a week as reported by different media and evaluate coverage for incidences of biased reporting. This will contribute to your understanding of objectivity and subjectivity that will help you maintain balance when considering what you write yourself.

11.3 Practise examining all sides of an argument. Choose a topic, perhaps one on which you have strong views (for example, a political matter, such as state support for university education; or an ethical one, such as vivisection or abortion). Write down the supporting arguments for different sides of the issue, focussing on your least-favoured option. This exercise will help you see all sides of a debate as a matter of course.

Further detailed information about the issues in this chapter can be found in McMillan and Weyers, 2013b. *How to improve your critical thinking and reflective skills*.

12

REFERRING TO SOURCE MATERIAL IN YOUR WRITING

How to cite and reference correctly to avoid plagiarism

Your ability to develop a plan and then draft your writing will depend on the extent of your reading and your use of critical thinking to assess the significance of the points that emerge from the various sources that you have studied. This chapter examines some of the strict conventions exist relating to acknowledging these sources in academic writing.

KEY TOPICS

→ Why citing the work of others is important

→ The mechanics of citation and referencing

→ The rationale of citation

→ How to cite the work in text, footnotes and endnotes

→ Quoting, summarising and paraphrasing

→ Avoiding plagiarism in your written work

KEY UNIVERSITY TERMS

Bibliographical   Citing/citation   Copyright   Paraphrasing
Plagiarism   Quoting   Reference list   Summarising

In **Step 9** of the 12-step process of writing (**Table 1.1**), you need to finalise your reference list. To ensure that you know how to do so appropriately, this chapter outlines the practical aspects of using source material in accordance with these conventions of citation and referencing.

Following these conventions is important in all academic writing since this validates your research into the topic and your understanding of evidence and different viewpoints. You also acknowledge the ideas of others in your writing; you are expected to respect their contribution in your work. This is called citation and involves identifying the author or source within your text. Full details of authors and bibliographical information are listed in a reference list usually found at the end of your text.

Different systems operate in – and across – universities. Sometimes these are based on conventions within a discipline or professional body. Sometimes because the style has been dictated by a publisher, this has, by default, become the accepted style for that subject or discipline.

You need to know four key things about citations and the references that relate to these, namely:

1 the reasons for referring to the work of others in their text

2 the mechanics of how to cite and reference properly

3 the rationale for citation and how to apply the rules within the context of their text

4 how to avoid plagiarising the work of others.

Definitions

Bibliography: a listing at the end of your work of all the books, journals, web and online materials that you have **read** as preparation for writing your paper. In this instance, you do not need to have referred to all sources directly in your text. Note that in some styles the word 'bibliography' is used instead of the term 'reference list' or 'references'.

Citation: the use of the idea presented by an author and expressed *in your own words* to support a point in your own work.

Quotation: the use of words drawn from the source you read. The words should remain faithful to the original.

Reference List (sometimes 'Works Listed' or 'Works Cited'): all the books, journals, web and online materials you have *referred to* in your paper.

WHY CITING THE WORK OF OTHERS IS IMPORTANT

Citations in your text contribute to validating your work as a serious piece of research. You need to give this information in order to:

1 acknowledge the use of other people's work so that their right to their intellectual property is recognised

2 state the sources from which you have borrowed text or information or ideas. You must do this even where you disagree with what was printed

3 help your reader (the marker) understand what influenced your thinking and how your argument/discussion was assembled. This will help them to form an opinion about your work

4 help your reader (the marker) to evaluate the extent of your reading. This may help them to assess the quality of your research and to advise you on further or more relevant reading

5 provide readers with sufficient information to enable them to consult the source materials for themselves, if they wish.

THE MECHANICS OF CITATION AND REFERENCING

Many systems of citation exist and some are used more frequently within the text in some disciplines than others. These can be classified into roughly four groups.

1 **Name/date style** – only uses the family name of the author and the date of publication.

2 **Name/page style** – uses name of author in the sentence introducing the point from the source with page number at the end of the sentence.

3 **Numerical style** – uses full size numerals inserted in brackets after the reported point and then lists these at the end of the work with full bibliographical information.

4 **Superscript numbering style** – inserts superscript in text at or near point being made from source; numbers relate to footnotes or endnotes giving publication details at the bottom of the page.

Sometimes the choice of citation style is dictated by your department and you will find this information in the course handbook. Where there is no particular recommendation, then you may wish to select a style that you find clearest and easiest to implement. Table 12.1 provides basic information about four styles of citation. To assist you in your choice, the table explains advantages and disadvantages. Note that guidance on layout of references in the final list can be prescriptive especially about spacing. The important thing is to be consistent in how you present the information and never mix different styles in the same list.

Table 12.1 **Choosing a citation style.** These styles apply to all forms of academic writing from essays and reports to theses.

Name/date style: Harvard	
Example	Smith (2012) suggests that students write only what they can write, not necessarily what they know. OR Students write only what they can write, not necessarily what they know (Smith, 2012).
Advantages	• Minimal typing, once-only entry in alphabetical order by author name in the reference list • Easy to identify contributors in a field from the citations shown in the text • Easy to make adjustments in the text and the reference list
Disadvantages	• Name/date references can be intrusive in the text • Not well suited to citing archive material e.g. historical documents which may not have full details sufficient to comply with the system
Name/page style: Modern Languages Association (MLA)	
Example	Smith suggests that students write only what they can write, not necessarily what they know (347). OR Students write only what they can write, not necessarily what they know (Smith 347).
Advantages	• Minimal typing as details are printed only once in alphabetical order by author name in the reference list, which makes it easy to locate the source information. • Easy to identify contributors in a field from citations shown in the text
Disadvantages	• Date of publication of source not in the text and not immediately evident in the reference list because of the position at the end of the reference. • Indentation of 'follow-on' lines in the reference list can give a 'ragged' appearance to the layout of the reference list
Numerical style: Vancouver	
Example	Smith suggests that students write only what they can write, not necessarily what they know (8).
Advantages	• Numbers are less intrusive in the text • Numbers are listed in numerical order at the end of the text, thus it is easy to locate the reference
Disadvantages	• No bibliographical information in the text, thus difficult to gauge significance of the sources • Cumbersome • Use of one number each time the source is used • Involves a considerable amount of checking and slows down the writing process
Superscript style: Harvard	
Example	Smith suggests that students write only what they can write, not necessarily what they know[8].
Advantages	• Numbering system is unobtrusive and does not interrupt the flow of the text • Use of 'op. cit' and 'ibid' in the referencing system saves retyping of bibliographical information
Disadvantages	• First mention of a source gives full details, subsequent references give only name/page in the footnote • More difficult to track the main contributors • Layout of footnote references differs from the bibliographical reference (if used) • Intensive checking to ensure that all superscript references are consistent after any changes

What information do I need to record for a citation and a reference?

Since citation systems differ, the information given within the citation in the text and the reference list are not consistent across styles. However, at reading and note-making stages it is important to record full bibliographical details so that, when including citations in your writing and creating your reference list, you can extract the information relevant to the style you have to use. Essential information should include:

Author(s) surname	Author(s) Initials	Date of publication	Title of book or article	Title of journal (if applicable)	Page numbers	Publisher	Place of publication

Note: Information varies according to whether the source is published by one author or multiple authors or under editorship. Titles of articles as well as the titles of the journals in which they appeared have to be given along with volume and page numbers. Publishing houses often merge and name changes occur; you should give the name that appears on the book source that you read. If a book has been printed in additional editions, then you also need to note the edition number (this may be important for the accuracy of content). How source information about website and online resources is recorded continues to evolve as each citation style develops its own style in this area. The need to give the date that a site was accessed seems to be common to all.

Software referencing packages

These can be used to fit your reference list to any of several conventions. However, it can be argued that the time taken to learn how to use such packages erodes the time that you have for writing. You could achieve a similar result by typing a list into a word-processed table that can then be easily sorted.

THE RATIONALE OF CITATION

Students can become over-absorbed with the layout of a reference list or the application of the citation style within their text, often neglecting to think about their reasons for including the citation in the first place.

Abbreviations used in citation and referencing

Some citation styles use certain abbreviations to save space within the citation or referencing format (note that Latin terms are printed in italics). Abbreviations commonly used include:

ed.	Editor or edition
et al.	And others (for multiple authors)
ibid.	In the same place
loc. cit.	In the same place as the previous citation for the same work
op. cit.	As earlier reference to the same work but not the immediately previous reference
p. or pp.	Page or pages

There has to be a good reason for including a citation in your text. You may want to relate your discussion to the literature sources, for example, because the author:

- presents overall coverage thus far of the topic within the wider literature as a preliminary to presenting their own contribution
- has conducted a critical analysis of the existing literature
- reports new or unchallenged evidence
- agrees with your point and provides evidence in support
- disagrees with your point and offers counter-argument.

HOW TO CITE THE WORK IN TEXT, FOOTNOTES AND ENDNOTES

In-text citation

Two methods are commonly used to introduce the source citation in your text. The layout depends on the citation style that you have elected to follow.

- **Information-prominent method.** Here the statement is regarded as being generally accepted within the field of study and the author's name and date of publication come at the end of the text relating to their work. For example:

Children express an interest in books and pictures from an early age (Murphy, 1995).

- **Author-prominent method.** Here the author and date of publication form part of the construction of the sentence. This formulation can be used with appropriate reporting words (see information box) to reflect a viewpoint. For example:

Murphy (2008) claimed that children as young as six months are able to follow a simple story sequence.

Footnote and endnote citation

In some disciplines, footnotes and endnotes, generally using superscript numbers, lead readers to the source of information. However, in other subjects, footnotes and endnotes are used simply to provide additional information, commentary or points of discussion about the content of the text. Footnotes generally appear at the bottom of the page where the link appears; endnotes are recorded in number order at the end of the body of work. Be guided by your course handbook or by the rules and conventions of the citation style you are required to use.

Reporting words

A considerable range of verbs can be used to report the views of others (usually in the past tense e.g. claimed, reported). Here are some examples.

- allege
- assert
- claim
- contend
- conjecture
- declare
- demonstrate
- explain
- found
- judge
- report
- show
- state
- surmise
- warn

Note that some of these words are 'stronger' than others and you need to consider carefully which you use so that they reflect your view of the reported work.

QUOTING, SUMMARISING AND PARAPHRASING

Citations should not just be randomly scattered through your text without reason. You need to make the connection between that source and the point that you wish to make by explaining why you think that particular piece of information is relevant to your discussion. You can do this by means of one of three language devices:

- Quoting in the text
- Summarising
- Paraphrasing

Quoting in the text

There are two possible ways of introducing quotations into your text (give the page reference in each case):

1 short quotation – exact words are placed within single quotation marks (inverted commas) within the sentence (e.g. Xxxx 'zzzzzzzz zzz zzzzzz zzzzz' (p. 000) xxx.).

2 longer quotation – usually 30 words or more. No quotation marks are used. In this case the status of the text as a quotation is indicated by the use of indentation within your own text and in single-line space; the preceding and following text should be in double or 1.5 line-spacing as directed in your guidelines. If you deliberately miss out some words from the original, then the 'gap' is represented by three dots (…) called ellipsis. For example:

xxxxxxx xxxx xxx xx xxx xxxxxxx xxx xx xxx xxxxxxx xxxxx xxx

xx xxxxx xxxx xxxxxxx:

…zzzz zzzz z zzzzz zzzzzzzzzzzz zzzz zz zzzz zzzzzzzzzzzzz zzzzzz zz zzzzzz zzzzzzzzz (author or source, page)

xxxxxxx xxxx xxx xx xxx xxxxxxx xxx xx xxx xxxxxxx xxxxx xx.

Summarising

In this method, you choose to provide an overview of the source material in general terms using your own words, that is, you provide the essence of the idea so that you can relate it to your own discussion and provide the appropriate citation within that summary. The best approach to this is as follows:

1 Read the topic and terminator paragraphs for main ideas of text (**Ch 5**).

2 Read the topic sentences of intervening paragraphs and allocate a defining term for each paragraph to identify main topic, point, argument or counter-argument. Create a list of these terms to give an overview of the text; highlight points of particular relevance to your own work.

3 Leave the task for a time and, on return, write down recollections without looking at the text or your list. Cross-reference recollections and your list, adding omissions to notes.

4 Using these expanded notes, remove unnecessary words or change the word order to create shorter sentences or phrases.

5 Start by creating an appropriate citation for the authors, identify the main theme and key points explaining how the main theme will form part of the discussion in your own text.

Paraphrasing

In this method, you condense the ideas from the source material in your own words but giving more detail than in summarising, that is, you explain the content more fully to provide supporting evidence for your own viewpoint. Again, providing the citation information appropriately within the text.

In both cases, technical terms can be retained, but otherwise different vocabulary and sentence structure are used to explain the key ideas from the original. An effective approach to this is as follows:

1 Read the text to establish general meaning (**Appendix 1**), that is, by reading topic sentences first of all (**Ch 5**).

2 Turn over the text and note down key ideas.

3 Re-read the text intensively for greater detail.

4 Turn over the text and, from memory, note points that support the key ideas. This encourages you to use your own words and makes you less dependent on the order or words from the text.

5 Note how you intend to use these ideas in your work.

6 Record bibliographical details for your reference list.

Table 12.2 gives contrasting examples of good and bad summarising and paraphrasing.

Paraphrase by starting at the end

Sometimes it is helpful when constructing paraphrased text to begin with the concluding idea of the text and work through the key ideas from that perspective rather than in the logic sequence of the original. In this way you are less likely to lapse into the pitfalls of word substitution, over-quotation or even plagiarism.

Table 12.2 Examples of summarising and paraphrasing

Original text:
E-books are a function of the internet era and make access to otherwise unattainable material possible to wide audiences. The globalisation of literature means that individual authors can present their work to a wider audience without incurring abortive publication costs. This facility constitutes a considerable threat to publishers of traditional books.   Source: Watt, W. (2006) *The demise of the book*. Dundee: Riverside Press. (p. 13)

Summarising

Poor model of summarising	Explanation	Good model of summarising
It has been suggested that '**e-books are a function of the internet era**' and that '**globalisation of literature**' allows authors to '**present their work to a wider audience**' without having to incur '**abortive publication costs**'.	*In this example, direct quotation (shown in bold) comprises 60 per cent of the total word count – this is excessive and could be regarded as a form of plagiarism. This fault is compounded because the writer has failed to give the source of the quotations.*	With the advent of e-books, individual authors are faced with new approaches to publication of their work (Watt, 2006).

Paraphrasing

Poor model	Explanation	Good model
E-books are part of the internet _age_ and allow people from all over the _globe_ to use them. This _means that writers show_ their _writing_ on the internet and so they _do not have such high publishing costs_. This _feature_ means that _publishers of old-fashioned books_ are _under threat_ (Watt, 2006).	*In this example, use of synonyms (underlined) in a superficial manner constitutes another form of plagiarism. Despite correctly citing the source, the writer has simply 'stolen' the essential meaning without engaging in any analysis or original thinking.*	Watt (2006) notes that there is concern amongst publishers of hard-copy printed books that the advent of e-books marks the end of their monopoly of the literature market, since authors can publish directly on the internet, thus avoiding publishing costs.

AVOIDING PLAGIARISM IN YOUR WRITTEN WORK

Plagiarism, using the work of others without acknowledgement, can be avoided. However, there are many misconceptions about plagiarism. Some plagiarism is blatant, some derives from these misconceptions.

For clarity, plagiarism occurs when writers:

- use the work of others as if it were their own, that is, without acknowledging the authorship
- copy the work of a fellow student (past or present) and present it as their own
- buy an essay from the internet or another person and present it as their own
- use words directly from the text but without quotation marks/with or without citation
- quote to such an extent that more than 10% of their text is derived from quotation, which means that there is little evidence of understanding or analysis in their work
- omit the citation and simply substitute words or re-arrange sentences. This may have been acceptable at earlier stages in your education, but it is not appropriate at university level
- cut and paste directly from the internet
- submit the same piece of work for two different assignments.

Avoiding plagiarism is simple. Do not do any of the things described in the above list. Instead, follow the advice given in the earlier part of this chapter.

How do I reference a source that I have read about in another text?

This situation refers to 'secondary referencing'. This approach is necessary when a writer needs to cite work that they have been unable to obtain or access themselves. This could be because the item is out of print or unavailable for other reasons. In this case, cite the text that you read yourself. In the text, following the Harvard style, it would look like:

- Russell (1958, cited in Crabbe, 1960) suggested that learning chess introduced problem-solving logic to primary school children.

- Learning chess in early school years has been recommended to introduce problem-solving logic to primary school children (Russell, 1958 cited in Crabbe, 1960).

Similarly, in your reference list, you would provide the details only of the book you read yourself.

Appendix 6.1 provides an example of how to lay out text following Harvard style and Appendix 6.2 shows how entries to a reference list should be laid out according to resource type. Information about additional styles is given in McMillan and Weyers (2013a).

PRACTICAL TIPS FOR USING SOURCE MATERIAL IN YOUR WRITING

Double check your 'original' ideas and viewpoints. If you have what you think is a novel idea do not simply accept that your brainwave is unique. It's common for people to forget the original source of an idea, which may resurface in their mind after many years and perhaps in a different context – this may have happened to you. Think carefully about possible sources that you may have forgotten about; ask others (such as your tutor) whether they have come across the idea before; and consult relevant texts, encyclopaedias or other sources including the internet to ensure that you have not derived the idea from elsewhere.

Assess the types of reporting words used in your discipline. Take a textbook or article in your area and identify the words that are typically used to introduce citations within these texts. This will give you some opportunity to expand the list of reporting verbs given in this chapter.

Avoid citing lecturers or lecture notes as sources to support your writing. As noted earlier in this book, lectures are intended to guide you towards further study, reflection and understanding. Therefore, if you cite what you heard in a lecture, this indicates that you have not acted as an independent thinker. This might mean that you would lose marks.

GO And now ...

12.1 Find out your school/department/university policy on plagiarism. This should describe the precise situations in which you might break the rules and may explain how plagiarism is detected. This can be achieved using software packages accessible to teaching staff, such as *Turnitin*™, which can scrutinise word-processed submissions and highlights text that is potentially copied. Note that the output of these programmes would always be moderated by a member of staff. Human recognition of plagiarism is always possible since markers will be familiar with the literature and recognise it embedded in student writing.

12.2 Compile your reference list as you go along. Simply create a table within your software package and type in the details immediately after you cite the source in the text. Doing this from time to time as you write saves you having to embark on a marathon of typing at the completion of the task. You will need to have made a decision about the citation and referencing style at an early stage in your writing.

12.3 Check out copyright information related to copying. A legal issue concerning plagiarism relates to copyright. Legislation and regulation cover the amount of photocopying or downloading of material that can be done by an individual. Information about this is usually available in the photocopier area in your university library. You should note the restrictions to ensure that your use of the work of others does not infringe these regulations.

Further detailed information covering the topics introduced in this chapter can be found in McMillan and Weyers, 2013a. *How to cite, reference and avoid plagiarism at university.*

13

PRESENTATION OF ACADEMIC ASSIGNMENTS

How to follow academic conventions in your written work

The presentation of your written work may be assessed directly and it may influence the way tutors view and assess the content. This chapter explains how to create a polished submission that follows the established standards of academic writing.

KEY TOPICS

→ Overall layout

→ Cover page

→ Main text

→ Citations and references

→ Quotes and formulae

→ Quoting numbers in text

→ Figures and tables

KEY UNIVERSITY TERMS

Analogy   Assignment   Citation   Legend   Qualitative
Quantitative   Quotation

Most marks for your academic assignments will be awarded for content, which depends on:

● activities that take place *before* you write, such as researching your sources, conducting experiments or analysing the literature (**Chs 1–5**)

● the way you express your ideas in writing (**Chs 15–17**).

As explained in **Chapters 8–12**, the effectiveness of the way you structure your writing contributes significantly to your final grade.

However, presentation can also affect how your work is perceived and assessed. This is the first aspect that can influence a reader and some marks may be directly or indirectly reserved for presentational features as appropriate to level and discipline. Lack of attention to these 'cosmetic' details can affect your marks adversely. Thus, by attending to layout and presentation you begin **Step 10** of the 12-step process in writing. This step is followed through in **Chapter 17** on editing and proof-reading.

A shrewd student will be aware of the presentational requirements *before* beginning to write and so will follow the conventions of presentation *as they write*. This saves considerable time at the reviewing, editing and proof-reading stage of the writing process when time may be short (**Ch 17**). To cover this and other aspects of reviewing, editing and proof-reading your work, you should aim to finish at least a day ahead of the submission date.

Why does good presentation matter?

- It may be an element of the assessment.
- It helps the marker understand what you have written.
- It shows that you adopt professional standards in your work.
- It demonstrates you have acquired important skills that will transfer to other subjects and, later, employment.

OVERALL LAYOUT

This will depend on the type of academic writing you have been asked to produce – an essay, report, summary or a case study, for example. An assignment like an essay could have a relatively simple structure: a cover page, the main essay text and a list of references. A lab report might be more complex, with a title page, abstract, introduction and sections for materials and methods, results, discussion/conclusion and references. Layouts for most types of assignment also vary slightly depending on discipline. You should research this carefully before you start to write up by consulting the course handbook or other regulations.

COVER PAGE

This is important to get right because it will create a good first impression. Your department may specify a cover-page design that is required for all submissions. If this is the case, then make sure that you follow the instructions closely, as the layout may have been constructed for a particular purpose. For example, it may aid anonymous marking or provide markers with a standard format for providing feedback.

If detailed instructions for a cover page are not given, then ensure that you provide your name and/or matriculation number at the head of your work. Where anonymous marking is applied, then your matriculation number only would be required. Add your course title and/or code. The tutor's name is also helpful. Give the assignment number and title of the assignment. The model layout in Figure 13.1 suggests one way to present the essential information neatly and clearly. Keep it simple: a cover sheet with fancy graphics will not add to your mark.

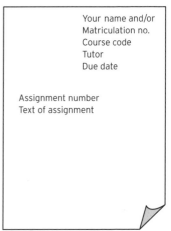

Figure 13.1 **A model cover-page layout**

MAIN TEXT

The majority of student assignments are word-processed and this may be a submission requirement. Using a word processor gives a more professional result and also makes the drafting and editing phases easier. Presentation features to consider include:

Font

There are two main choices: serif types, with extra strokes at the end of the main strokes of each letter, and sans serif types, without these strokes (see Figure 13.2). The type to use is usually left to personal preference. More likely to be specified is the point size (pt) of the font, which will probably be 11 or 12 point for ease of reading.

You should avoid using elaborate font types as generally they will not help the reader to assimilate what you have written. For the same reason, you should not use too many forms of emphasis. In general, choose *italics* or **bold** and stick with one only. Symbols are often used in academic work and in Microsoft Word can be added using the 'Insert > Symbol' menu.

Serif font
Times roman 11 pt
Times roman 12 pt
Times roman 14 pt

Sans serif font
Arial 11 pt
Arial 12 pt
Arial 14 pt

Figure 13.2 Examples of the main types of font at different point sizes

Margins

A useful convention is for left-hand margins to be 4 cm and the right-hand margins 2.5 cm. This allows space for the marker's comments and ensures that the text can be read if a left-hand binding is used.

Line spacing

It is easier to read text that is spaced at least at 1.5 to 2 lines apart. Some markers like to add comments as they read the text and this leaves them space to do so. The exception is where you wish to use long quotations. These should be indented and typed in single-line spacing (**Ch 12**).

Paragraphs

The key thing to remember about layout is to make good use of the 'white space' by laying out your paragraphs clearly and consistently. Some people prefer the indentation method, where the paragraphs (except the first one) begin on the fourth character space from the left-hand margin (Figure 13.3a). Others prefer the blocked paragraph style, that is, where all paragraphs begin on the left-hand margin but are separated by a double-line space (Figure 13.3b). The space between paragraphs should be roughly equivalent to a missing line. In Microsoft Word these aspects can be controlled using the 'Format > Paragraph' menu.

Sub-headings

In some disciplines use of sub-headings is acceptable or even favoured, though in others these 'signpost' strategies are discouraged. It is best to consult your tutor or course handbook about this if you are uncertain. Sub-headings are usually in bold. They may also be numbered.

Punctuation

Standard punctuation applies to all types of academic writing and is dealt with in detail in **Appendix 7**.

Word count

You may be asked to work to a word count and tips for doing this are provided in **Ch 17**. If you greatly exceed this limit, this will almost certainly impact on your presentation as you will confront the reader with too much information and will probably not be writing crisply and concisely.

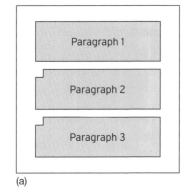

(a)

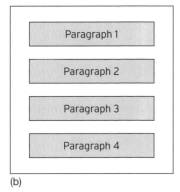

(b)

Figure 13.3 Types of paragraph layout. (a) indented and (b) fully justified (blocked). Note that in the indented model, by convention the first paragraph in any section is not indented.

CITATIONS AND REFERENCES

The reasons for citation and style of citing the work of others were covered in detail in **Chapter 12**. This is an important academic convention that you must observe to avoid plagiarism (**Ch 12**). Providing a reference list is, therefore, standard practice and, for this reason, markers may deduct marks if you omit one.

If in doubt, consult your course handbook or your lecturer.

Examples

The following is an example of a citation:

According to Smith (2005), there are three reasons why aardvark tongues are long.

The following is an example of a reference:

Smith, J. V., 2005. Investigation of snout and tongue length in the African aardvark *(Orycteropus afer). Journal of Mammalian Research,* 34; 101–32.

QUOTATIONS AND FORMULAE

Quotations and formulae can be integrated into the text when short, but are usually presented as a 'special' type of paragraph when long. In both cases, the source, date of publication and page reference are provided after the quotation (**Ch 12**). Some disciplines also require a page number for the quotation.

- **Short quotations** are integrated within the sentence and are placed within single inverted commas. Quotations within the quote are in double inverted commas (**Appendix 7** and Figure 13.4).

- **Long quotations** are usually 30 or more words of prose or more than two lines of poetry. They are indented by five character spaces from the left margin. No quotation marks are necessary unless there

The cultural values identifiable in one minority group create what has been called the 'invisible clamour' (Henze, 1990, p. 53) as they conflict with those of the dominant culture.

Figure 13.4 **How to present a short quotation in text form**

are quotation marks used in the text you are quoting (Figure 13.5).

Some disciplines, for example, English Literature and Law, have very specific rules for the way in which quotations are to be laid out and referenced. In such cases, consult your course handbook or ask for guidance from a tutor.

Short formulae or equations can be included in text, but they are probably better presented on a separate line and indented, thus

$$\alpha + 4\beta / \eta^2 \pi = 0 \qquad \text{(Eqn. 13.1)}$$

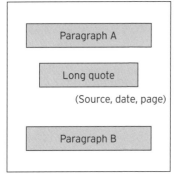

Figure 13.5 How to present a long quote, shown in outline form

Where a large number of formulae are included, they can be numbered for ease of cross-reference, as shown above.

QUOTING NUMBERS IN TEXT

Adopt the following rules:

- in less formal writing, spell out numbers from one to ten and use figures for 11 and above; in formal writing, spell out numbers from one to a hundred and use figures beyond this
- spell out high numbers that can be written in two words ('six hundred'). With a number like 4,200,000, you also have the choice of writing '4.2 million'
- always use figures for dates, times, currency or to give technical details ('5-amp fuse')
- always spell out numbers that begin sentences (Twenty children ...), indefinite numbers (hundreds of soldiers) or fractions (seven-eighths) and hyphenate numbers (thirty-five) and fractions (two-thirds) appropriately.

FIGURES AND TABLES

You may be expected to support your academic writing with visual material or data, and it is important that you do so in a fashion that best helps the reader to assimilate the information. You must also follow any specific presentational rules that apply in your subject area.

Figures

The academic convention is to include a wide range of visual material under the term 'Figure' ('Fig.' for short, although this is not approved in some subjects). This includes graphs, diagrams, charts, sketches, pictures and photographs, although in some disciplines and contexts photographs may be referred to as plates. Here is a set of guidelines to follow when including figures in an assignment:

- all figures should be referred to in the text. There are 'standard' formulations for doing this, such as 'Figure 4 shows that ...'; or '... results for one treatment were higher than for the other (see Fig. 2)'. Find what is appropriate from the literature or texts in your subject area

- you should always number the figures in the order they are referred to in the text. If you are including the figures within the main body of text (usually more convenient for the reader) then they should appear at the next suitable position in the text after the first time of mention. At the very least this will be after the paragraph that includes the first citation, but more normally will be at the top of the following page

- try to position your figures at the top or bottom of a page, rather than sandwiched between blocks of text. This looks neater and makes the text easier to read

- each figure should have a legend, which will include the figure number, a title and some text (often a key to the symbols and line styles used). The convention is for figure legends to appear below each figure. Your aim should be to make each figure self-contained.

Inserting figures in text

Integrated suites of 'office' software allow you to insert the graphs you produced using the spreadsheet program into text produced with the word-processing program. The two programs can even be linked so that changes on the spreadsheet data automatically appear in the graph within the word-processed file. Consult the manual or 'Help' facility to find out how to do this. In MS Word, digital photographs can be inserted using the 'Insert > Picture > From File' command.

That is, a reader who knows the general subject area should be able to work out what your figure shows, without reference to other material. Figure 13.6 shows the basic components of the 'graph' type of figure and its layout.

Choosing the right *type* of figure to display information is an art in itself. Although there are technical reasons why some forms of data should be presented in particular ways (for example, proportional data in a pie chart rather than a line chart), your main focus should always be on selecting a method that will best help the reader assimilate the information presented. Jones, Reed and Weyers (2007) or the 'Chart Wizard' in the Microsoft Office Excel spreadsheet program are possible starting points for exploring the range of possibilities.

When presenting individual figures, clarity should be your main aim – ensuring, for example, that the different slices of a pie chart or the lines and symbols in a graph are clearly distinguishable from one another. Consistency is also important, so you should use the same line or shading for the same entity in all your figures (for example, hollow symbols for 'controls'). The widespread availability of colour printers should help with this, but some departments may insist on the use of black and white, since this was the convention when colour printing was prohibitively expensive. If you are using colour, keep it 'tasteful' and remember that certain colour

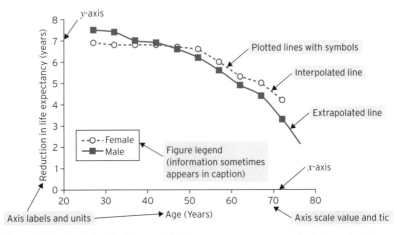

Figure 89 **A standard plotted curve.** This figure type uses *x-y* axes and points and lines to illustrate the relationship between two variables. *Source*: Data modified from Rogers, R.G. and Powell-Griner E., 1991. Life expectancies of cigarette smokers and non-smokers in the United States. *Soc. Sci. Med.*, 32, 1151-9.

Figure **13.6 The basic components of a graph**

The norm is to put the controlled variable or category of measurement on the *x*-axis (horizontal axis) and the measured variable on the *y*-axis (vertical axis):

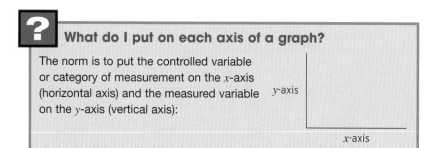

y-axis

x-axis

combinations are not easily differentiated by some readers. Take great care to ensure that the quantity plotted and its units are provided for all axes.

Tables

These are used to summarise large amounts of information, in particular where a reader might be interested in some of the detail of the data. Tables are useful for qualitative textual information but numerical data can also be presented, especially if they relate to a discontinuous qualitative variable (for example, the population sizes and occupation breakdown of various geographical regions).

Tables generally include a number of columns (vertical) and rows (horizontal). By analogy with figures, the convention is to put the controlled or measured variable on the column headers (horizontal) and to place the measured variable or categories of measurement in the rows (vertical). Do not forget to include the units of the information listed if this is relevant.

The rules for presenting tables are very similar to those for figures, with the important difference that a table legend should appear above the table. It is quite common to note exceptions and other information as footnotes to tables. Figure 13.7 shows the basic components of tables and their layouts.

Figure or table?

In certain cases it may be possible to present the same data set as a figure or as a table. The first rule in such cases is never do both – choose the method that best suits your data and the target reader. An important criterion is to decide which will help the reader best to assimilate the information. If the take-home message is best shown visually, then a figure might better; whereas, if details and numerical accuracy are important, then a table might be more suitable.

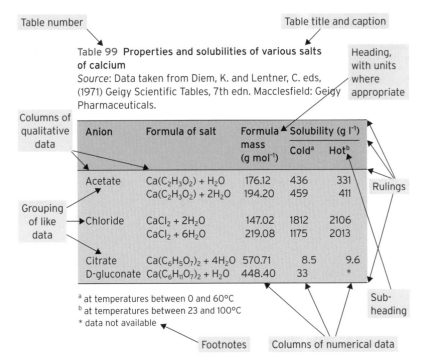

Table number → Table 99 **Properties and solubilities of various salts of calcium**
Source: Data taken from Diem, K. and Lentner, C. eds, (1971) Geigy Scientific Tables, 7th edn. Macclesfield: Geigy Pharmaceuticals.

Table title and caption

Heading, with units where appropriate

Columns of qualitative data

Grouping of like data

Rulings

Sub-heading

Anion	Formula of salt	Formula mass (g mol^{-1})	Solubility (g l^{-1})	
			Cold[a]	Hot[b]
Acetate	$Ca(C_2H_3O_2) + H_2O$	176.12	436	331
	$Ca(C_2H_3O_2) + 2H_2O$	194.20	459	411
Chloride	$CaCl_2 + 2H_2O$	147.02	1812	2106
	$CaCl_2 + 6H_2O$	219.08	1175	2013
Citrate	$Ca(C_6H_5O_7)_2 + 4H_2O$	570.71	8.5	9.6
D-gluconate	$Ca(C_6H_{11}O_7)_2 + H_2O$	448.40	33	*

[a] at temperatures between 0 and 60°C
[b] at temperatures between 23 and 100°C
* data not available

Footnotes

Columns of numerical data

Figure 13.7 The basic components of a table. Note that shading is included here to emphasise the heading and data sections and would not usually be present.

PRACTICAL TIPS FOR PRESENTING YOUR WORK

Don't let grammatical and stylistic errors spoil your work. It is a waste of effort to concentrate on presentation without also ensuring that you have ironed out minor grammatical errors at the review and proof-reading stages (**Appendices 7–10**).

Plan your time well if handwriting your submissions. Make sure that you leave sufficient time to copy out your draft neatly and legibly. Write on only one side of the paper – this makes it easier to read, and if you make a significant error you will only have to rewrite a single sheet.

Adopt standard word-processing layout conventions. Adopting the following guidelines will ensure a neat, well-spaced presentation:

● one character space after the following punctuation – full stop, comma, colon, semicolon, closing inverted commas (double and single), question mark and exclamation mark

- no character space after apostrophes in a 'medial' position e.g. it's, men's, monkey's
- no indentation of paragraphs (that is, blocked style)
- one standard line space between paragraphs
- left-justified text
- italicised letters for foreign words and titles of books, journals and papers
- headings in same font size as text, but bold.

Adopt figure and table styles from the literature. If you have doubts about the precise style or arrangement of figures and tables, follow the model shown in texts or journal articles from your subject area. Also, check whether relevant instructions are published in the course handbook.

Don't automatically accept the graphical output from spreadsheets and other programs. These are not always in the 'correct' style. For example, the default output for many charts produced by the Microsoft Office Excel spreadsheet includes a grey background and horizontal gridlines, neither of which is generally used. It is not difficult to alter these parts of the chart, however, and you should learn how to do this from manuals or the 'Help' facility.

(GO) And now . . .

13.1 Check for 'white' space. Look critically at your text to identify whether you have used paragraphing effectively. A useful 'trick' is to reduce the 'zoom' function on the toolbar to 25%. Your written pages will then appear in multiples on the screen which will allow you to see the overall distribution of 'white' space and length of paragraphs. This may suggest some alterations to make your text more reader-friendly.

13.2 'Personalise' your work. In many institutions the convention is for students to submit written work with only their matriculation mark as an identifier. This is done in order to facilitate anonymous marking. However, if your pages become detached for some reason, then it may be difficult for the marker to ensure that all your pages are actually included in the document that they mark. Thus, you should do three very basic things: firstly, staple all sheets together (paper clips fall off); secondly, using the View/header-footer function, insert your matriculation number in the footer, in a smaller font than the main text if you wish it to be less obtrusive; and, thirdly, insert page numbers in the footer also. This means that each page is identifiable as yours and will remain in sequence. If you are not in the habit of doing these things, then create an assignment writing template in which you insert the matriculation/ identity number and page numbers. You can then use this routinely for all future written coursework.

13.3 Check out positioning of tables and figures. Look back at previous assignments to identify whether you have been consistent and correct in positioning tables and figures.

14

WHAT MARKERS LOOK FOR WHEN ASSESSING WRITTEN WORK

How markers grade your academic writing

To be successful in processing information and creating well-written text, new academic writers need to understand the mindset of those who set and grade their work. This chapter explores different dimensions of what markers look for in written submissions – although they do not always intimate this agenda to students.

KEY TOPICS

→ Taking account of course guidance material

→ How written assignments are graded

→ What markers are looking for in terms of presentation

→ What markers are looking for in terms of structure

→ What markers are looking for in terms of content

→ What will lower you marks

→ How coursework feedback can help to improve your future grades

KEY UNIVERSITY TERMS

Anonymous marking   Brief   External examiner
Feedback   Formative assessment   Learning objective
Learning outcome   Marking criteria   Marking scheme
Primary source   Secondary source   Syllabus

When they assign a grade to your work, markers are looking for a relevant response to the set task. In particular, they will be looking for features that distinguish your work as competent and appropriate to your level of study within the course or module you are taking. As noted in **Chapter 13**, these relate to three dimensions of writing: presentation, structure, content.

Therefore, the marker will assess the quality of your response to a task by reference to explicit and implicit marking criteria that relate to these three dimensions of your writing. Knowing what is expected of you in relation to your writing is essential prior to and whilst writing; it acts also as the basis of your understanding of any future feedback you receive on your graded work. Thus, this chapter introduces **Step 11** in the 12-step process of writing (**Table 1.1**) on responding to feedback by raising your awareness of how your work will be judged.

TAKING ACCOUNT OF COURSE GUIDANCE MATERIAL

You can find out about the broader criteria against which your work will be judged by looking more closely at your course guide or handbook. As noted in previous chapters, course guides and handbooks are often provided in hard copy. Where this is not the case, these may be posted on your course module within the course website or your institution's virtual learning environment. They usually provide generic and syllabus information.

Generic information

- assessment or reporting scales for assignments (often with grading criteria)
- particular citation and referencing formats
- information about word limits (and whether appendices are included in the word count)
- penalties for being below or above the permitted word count
- presentation and submission information
- penalties for late submission
- advice on writing style and conventions that may apply to that discipline.

Syllabus information and learning objectives or outcomes

To understand more particularly what the marker is looking for, you need to look at two more detailed parts of the course guide – the course syllabus and the related learning objectives (sometimes called 'outcomes'). In an ideal world, the learning objectives should relate to the way the topic is assessed. Depending on how the syllabus is structured and delivered, you may find that the objectives are outlined for the whole course, or that each theme within the syllabus has its own learning objectives, or both. Although some learning objectives are worded so that they do not provide detailed guidance, properly constructed learning objectives will give you a well-defined 'steer' on what the markers will be looking for in assignments, particularly if you map these on to the elements from the courses that are relevant to the writing task you have been set.

HOW WRITTEN ASSIGNMENTS ARE GRADED

Many students may be unaware of the events that lead to a grade being given to their work. However, it is important to understand this process if you wish to meet the expectations of the markers and be awarded a good mark. Here are some of the questions you should be considering:

- **Who grades your work?** The person who grades/marks your work is not always the academic who delivers the lecture content of the course. However, the marker will have an expertise in the discipline and be well-acquainted with the theme of the assignment. To ensure that fairness is applied to the grading system, papers may be 'double-marked'. This means that the scripts are marked by a second marker, generally from within the department. If the assignment is critical to a degree classification, or if there has been a difference between the grades allocated by the first and second markers, the paper may be sent to the external examiner for adjudication.

- **How do markers decide on your grade?** A number of factors will contribute to deciding your grade, but these may differ from subject to subject and assignment to assignment. To a certain extent, all markers reach their decision about a grade intuitively, based on their professional expertise as academics. However, to ensure that their decision is objective and that students are treated fairly and equally, markers will often refer to marking scales reflecting a list of generalised (departmental) marking criteria, such as those shown in Tables 14.1 and 14.2. In some cases, and especially where double-marking occurs, these may be further refined into a marking scheme for a specific question detailing what proportion of marks will be given to particular aspects or elements of your submission.

Marking criteria

These criteria are defined in course handbooks and explain what has to be achieved in order to attain particular grades. They differ from module to module, discipline to discipline and level to level. Thus, it is important to read them with care to identify the standards you hope to reach. In the top band for a module assignment, such criteria might state that assessed work should:

- contain all the information required with no, or very few, errors
- show evidence of reading from relevant literature and use it effectively in the answer
- address the task showing an understanding of all its nuances
- include little or no irrelevant material
- demonstrate full understanding of the topic within a wider context
- show good critical and analytical appraisal of the issues
- contain evidence of sound independent thinking
- express ideas clearly and concisely
- use appropriate written structure and a good standard of English
- present diagrams, where required, that are detailed and relevant.

- **Why is anonymous marking used?** To ensure further that there is no bias in assessment, anonymous marking is often used. The identity of the student is masked, possibly by use of personal identification or matriculation numbers. Thus, your identity as creator of the text is unknown so that gender, ethnicity, age or academic record cannot influence the grading. However, the identity of the marker will normally be shown on the feedback sheet or note at the end of your script. This can be advantageous because it allows you to be able to speak directly with the marker about weaknesses or errors in your work, thus personalising feedback.

- **What do grades mean?** Currently, each university sets its own grading scheme broadly based on what is called the 'honours classification', that is, the division of degrees into First Class, Upper Second Class, Lower Second Class and Third Class. At lower levels of study, these classifications do not generally apply, but students and staff tend to think of work as falling within these categories. Tables 14.1 and 14.2 show some different versions of the scales that are used to grade students' work in terms of the honours classification.

How do I know if I've got the right answer?

Clearly, if the assignment requires the manipulation of number, equations or other technical calculations, there will be an answer that is correct. In other instances in academic assignments there are no 'right' or 'wrong' answers – only a range of good answers that can be as varied as the number of answers submitted. Nor should the paper you submit be an echo of what you think that your lecturer wants to read. As a rule of thumb, provided that your answer is presented logically and presents sound evidence to support your viewpoint or approach, then it will be judged on its merits – whether the marker agrees or disagrees with you.

WHAT MARKERS ARE LOOKING FOR IN TERMS OF PRESENTATION

Lecturers frequently mark many assignments and there is a considerable volume of reading involved in order to assess these. Therefore, they are looking for:

- neatly presented assignments with an uncluttered layout as described in **Chapter 13**.
- ideas that are expressed clearly in good prose that is easily understood and uses the terminology appropriate to the subject.

To help you become more aware of the aspects you should be paying attention to, the checklist in column 1 of Table 14.3 shows some of the presentational features taken into account in the assessment of written work (**Ch 17**).

Presentation, structure and content

These three elements are interdependent, but experience suggests that poor presentation can often act as a barrier to understanding and can lose you marks. If readers cannot read the document because of poor layout or language use, for example, then they will struggle to follow the structure of the document and any argument it might contain. Similarly, if the structure is also poorly framed and thus unclear, then the content is going to be difficult to recognise. It is for these reasons that the presentation, structure and content are listed in that order.

Table 14.1 Numerical (percentage) marking scale with sample marking criteria for different grade classifications. Institutions vary about how coursework is graded. However, the typical marking criteria shown below will have some kind of correspondence with the system that applies in your institution and you should be able to find this information in your course handbook or guide.

Honours classification	Grade	Numerical mark	Marking criteria
First Class Honours	Grade A	70–100% (note that in some universities, this grade is split into two bands)	Work at this level will show an outstanding command of the material, a high level of the awareness of issues, developments and critical dimensions of the subject material. Evidence of original thinking and analysis will be apparent. In work of this standard, clear relationships between the topic and the wider context of the discipline will be drawn. Citation to the body of extant literature will be of a high standard.
Upper Second Class Honours	Grade B	60–69%	Work shows a good level of knowledge and analysis with critical appraisal of key issues supported by appropriate reference to the literature. It contains sophisticated argument and logical appraisal presented to a high standard.
Lower Second Class Honours	Grade C	50–59%	Work shows sound knowledge of subject material. Written response demonstrates an imbalance in favour of description rather than deeper critical thinking. Although some analysis present, this lacks sophistication.
Third Class Honours	Grade D	40–49%	Work shows limited evidence of knowledge and understanding of the subject material. Lack of analysis and evaluation of information and evidence. Reliance on reiteration of factual material and descriptive or narrative presentation of answer.
Fail	Grade F	35–39%	Work shows inadequate understanding of the task. Lack of coherent argument supported by use and interpretation of evidence drawn from the relevant literature.
Clear Fail	Ungraded	0–34%	Work shows little knowledge of the subject and no application to set task. Weak or no argument constructed. Plagiarism may be evident. Weak expression and use of language relevant to the discipline.

Table 14.2 A typical alpha-numeric marking scale, with corresponding aggregation scale used when combining elements of assessment.

Descriptor	Reporting Scale	Aggregation Scale	Corresponding Honours classification
Excellent	A1	21	First Class
	A2	20	
	A3	19	
Very good	B1	18	Upper Second Class (2.1)
	B2	17	
	B3	16	
Good	C1	15	Lower Second Class (2.2)
	C2	14	
	C3	13	
Satisfactory	D1	12	Third Class
	D2	11	
	D3	10	
Marginal fail	MF	9	Marginal fail
Clear fail	CF	6	Clear fail
Bad fail	BF	2	Bad fail
		0	

WHAT MARKERS ARE LOOKING FOR IN TERMS OF STRUCTURE

The structure of a piece of writing is important both to convey your understanding of the issues related to the topic and to outline your response to the aspect you have been asked to consider. Markers want to see:

● appropriate structure at sentence, paragraph and text level. Thus, it is important not only to ensure that sentences are concise and well-structured, but also that paragraphs are coherent and well-ordered within an appropriate academic format (**Ch 9** and **Ch 16**).

Table 14.3 Checklist relating to typical marking criteria. Relevant chapters in this book are shown within the cells.

Presentation	Structure	Content
❑ **Writing style:** should be • objective • formal as appropriate to academic writing • clear, correct, standard English with no truncated text messaging or other inappropriate abbreviations. (Ch] 10)	❑ **Logic of writing:** your writing should be planned carefully so it has a logical structure. The construction of sentences and paragraphs should contribute to the overall cohesion of the text. Poorly constructed sentence-level errors will make the text difficult to understand and may hamper the reader's comprehension. (Chs 9, 10, 15 and 16)	❑ **Quality of knowledge:** your writing should reflect: • an understanding of the range of module/course themes and your ability to make connections across topics • reading from the source material in addition to that presented in lectures. (Chs 2–6, 10 and 11)
❑ **Printed format:** practice varies from institution to institution, but, generally, work is word-processed and printed. You need to follow standard typing conventions such as spacing, justification and punctuation. If work is hand-written, print neatly and never use capitals throughout. (Ch 14 and Appendix 7)	❑ **Logic of discussion or argument:** evidence should be organised in support of the viewpoint but expressed in ways that avoid making value judgements. (Chs 9, 11,12 and 15)	❑ **Relevance:** the text should relate to the aspect of the topic defined by the task brief. If you write too much general material and fail to tackle the deeper, more complex issues, then this will have a negative impact on your grade. (Ch 6 and Chs 8–11)

□ **Spelling:** word processor spell-checking functions are not foolproof, so you also need to read your work over, paying particular attention, for example, to words that sound the same but have different spelling or words that are specific to your subject and that may have been misspelt in the text.

(Appendix 8)

□ **Grammar:** your word processor may indicate 'errors' of grammar (as well as mis-spelling) by underlining them. Check each of these, but note that often the diagnosed 'errors' are only suggestions for you to consider in context. For example, use of the passive, although often highlighted, is acceptable in academic writing and thus alteration may be unnecessary.

(Appendices 9 and 10)

□ **Relationship to literature:** in many disciplines, the line of argument that you need to construct should relate to key works in existing literature. You will be given credit for making these connections within your text, being careful, of course, to avoid plagiarism. If you fail to make these links or fail to explain why you are making them, then your work is weakened.

(Ch 12)

□ **Use of tables, diagrams, graphs or figures:** some subjects routinely require evidence to be presented in a visual format. If you need to demonstrate evidence in this way, ensure that visuals are labelled appropriately and are integrated into the text in a logical manner close to the text that explains their content. This contributes to the cohesion of your argument and the structure of your text.

(Ch 13)

□ **Critical thinking:** your writing must demonstrate an ability to analyse and synthesise complex ideas. At these higher levels of study, you need to demonstrate some ability to construct an original argument.

(Ch 11)

□ **Use of primary sources:** in some subjects the ability to analyse and evaluate material from primary sources will set your work apart from that of others as significant and worthy of a higher grade.

(Chs 11 and 12)

- writing with an identifiable and coherent introduction. Well-written work will help the reader understand the structure of the writing that follows and so will attract a higher mark.

- a main body where the points are signposted clearly. Guiding the reader, for example, through the analysis of causal relationships, a problem, or comparisons and contrasts will create a logic within your paper.

- a tightly summarised analytical conclusion. Completing the work with a coherent review of key points will mean that the marker is in a good position to assess the overall construction of the argument and more likely to reach a positive evaluation (**Chs 9, 11** and **15**).

The checklist in Column 2 of Table 14.3 shows some of the structural considerations taken into account in marking criteria for written work. **Chapters 8, 9, 15** and **Appendices 4** and **5** present structural models, and **Chapter 16** and **Appendices 9** and **10** explain how to create effective sentences and paragraphs.

WHAT MARKERS ARE LOOKING FOR IN TERMS OF CONTENT

The content of a piece of writing demonstrates your ability to select the relevant (and thus reject the irrelevant). When you present your analysis of the topic, markers want to see:

- a sound arrangement of selected facts and concepts. They are looking for factual knowledge and understanding of concepts, but not a script that is merely a list of facts (**Ch 2** and **Ch 11**).

- evaluation of knowledge, showing deeper-level understanding. The content of your script has to show analysis of evidence that supports your case. It should not be simply a description or narrative based on lecture notes or information gathered from the internet. In short you have to show an ability to think critically (**Ch 11**).

- reference to the relevant literature on the topic. At university level, you need to support your analysis with citations from a variety of primary and secondary sources using a recognised citation and system (**Ch 12**).

- good paraphrasing of ideas. Use of the ideas of others is acceptable, but expressed in your own words, and cited appropriately to support your response to the task (**Ch 12**).

WHAT WILL LOWER YOUR MARKS

Any number of aspects might lower your marks. Although the following list is not comprehensive, it may alert you to some of the things to avoid.

- Incorrect facts. Giving information which is wrong, out of date or inaccurate can diminish the strength of your discussion (**Chs 2–7** and **Ch 11**).

- Over-quotation. Scripts that rely too heavily on direct quotation or simply reformulate the wording of the original by changing a few words from the original text (**Ch 12**).

- 'Name-dropping'. Scripts which refer to authorities in the subject area but do not provide explanation as to the significance of their contributions or viewpoint (**Ch 12**).

- Rambling text. Submissions that make it difficult to follow the writer's train of thought (**Chs 8–12**).

- Incoherence. Submissions that come across as imprecise and muddled are often those where the writing style is vague for a variety of grammatical reasons (**Ch 16** and **Appendices 9** and **10**).

- Narrative script. A descriptive piece of writing that provides a sequential account of events without any evident analysis will probably indicate shallow thinking. This approach may reflect limited reading and little understanding of the relative importance of events or steps in a process that marks deeper-level thought (**Ch 11**).

- Poor editing and/or proof-reading. In some institutions marks will be deducted for repeated errors or sloppy proof-reading; in others, this is not the policy. Whatever your context, by ensuring that your work is presented correctly, you will encourage your marker into a frame of mind that perceives your work in a positive light (**Chs 13** and **17**).

HOW COURSEWORK FEEDBACK CAN HELP TO IMPROVE YOUR FUTURE GRADES

Feedback from your lecturers should indicate where you could improve your written work for subsequent assignments and exams (**Chs 18** and **19**). If the comments are unclear, or you cannot understand why you received the grade you did, then ask the marker or another tutor to provide additional comments or explanation. Most will respond helpfully to a polite request. You should use this information to create an action plan for future work. This might involve consulting and acting on some of the material in later chapters of this book, for example.

PRACTICAL TIPS FOR IMPROVING YOUR GRADES

Create glossaries. Compile a glossary (word list) of subject-specific terms that will probably be used in each new writing task and refer to them as you write to ensure that you are not guilty of mis-spelling or misuse of jargon.

Study the writing of your lecturers. Lecturers often provide handouts of their lectures. Apart from reviewing the content of such notes, study the way in which they have been written. This may introduce you to vocabulary, modes of expression and style that you might be able to use as a guide for your own writing. This would help you to meet the standards that your lecturer – in marker mode – would value.

Take notice of written feedback on your work. The person who graded your work will have given some pointers about where the strengths and weaknesses lay in your submission. Try to build further on the strengths and make deliberate efforts to act on suggestions of how you could improve on weaker aspects of your writing.

Take note of guidance you are given about writing for academic purposes. Advice on writing may be available at different times. You will probably find some guidance on writing in your subject area in your course handbook. Sometimes lecturers or tutors include some advice on written submissions in lectures or tutorials. You will also find that most universities offer support for writing in workshops or one-to-one tutorials. Taking note of what you read or hear and of what you could access through the specialist writing services in your university will mean that you can take active steps to meet the standards that markers would like to see in your writing.

GO And now ...

14.1 Check through the grading scales and marking criteria that apply in your university or department/school. These should be published online or in your course handbook. If you have already had work assessed, then reflect on ways in which you could improve your grade in the light of these criteria and the information in this chapter.

14.2 Establish your institution/school policy on anonymous marking. Sometimes this applies only to end of year examinations and not to coursework. Knowing what applies in your situation could be helpful if you want to discuss your work with teaching staff.

14.3 Go through Table 14.3 and reflect on how your writing would align with the checklists for presentation, structure and content. Knowing what is expected of you in your writing should give you some targets that you can set yourself in terms of developing your writing for academic purposes. Use this checklist when you are working on your next writing assignment to ensure that you cover as many of the points as possible to help you gain good grades.

WRITING TECHNIQUE – HOW TO
PLAN AND WRITE FOR ASSESSMENT

15

PLANNING YOUR WRITING ASSIGNMENTS

How to reflect on and organise your response to the task

From earlier chapters you will have become more aware of the principles of planning within an academic format, the skills of critical thinking, the methods of citing other sources and what markers expect of your writing when they grade your work. This chapter moves on to the reality of composing text by planning and writing according to typical structural approaches.

KEY TOPICS

→ Reflecting on the topic

→ Planning your writing

→ Adopting a structural approach

→ Expanding your outline

KEY UNIVERSITY TERMS

Lateral thinking

Examples of written assignments at university include essays, reports, project dossiers, short-answer mini-essays, case studies or dissertations. For longer pieces of writing, especially those that will count towards a module or degree mark, you will need to approach the task in a focussed manner. The 12-step writing process modelled in **Chapter 1** takes you from identifying what the assignment requires you to do, researching and evaluating relevant material in the context of the task you have been set and mapping this on to the three-element outline of introduction, main body and conclusion (**Steps 1–7** in **Chapters 1–11**). Later chapters (**Chs 12–14**) provide insights into how your work is evaluated.

This chapter briefly reviews and draws together these seven steps as the foundation for examining the structural approaches that you might need to apply to the construction of the draft of your first assignment.

REFLECTING ON THE TOPIC

Returning briefly to **Step 6** that requires you to reflect on your topic, you will recall that you need to:

- return to the task and analyse the topic, its aspect(s) and restriction(s) more thoroughly (**Ch 8**). This step is important because students often mis-read the task and, although they may submit a good piece of work, their response may miss the precise focus of the assignment

- create a concept 'map' of the topic (**Figure A2.5** for a model). To do this, you need to write down as many related aspects as you can in a free-flowing diagram. At this stage, you might be seeing patterns or groups of ideas that will influence your final response

- revisit the instruction word and, without consulting any notes or reading that you have done, consider how this applies to your initial response to the task. This may seem to be a strange approach, but these immediate thoughts are principally your own 'take' on the topic. The most important aspect is that you are beginning to exercise your critical thinking skills by analysing what you think is important about this subject (**Ch 11**)

- start asking yourself questions. This may help you to focus on what is important to your topic. For example:
    - Who are the key actors in a sequence of events?
    - What important or necessary factors explain particular situations?
    - What evidence or explanations support a particular viewpoint?
    - What patterns can be identified, for example, covering short-, medium- and long-term factors?

- build up an understanding of different perspectives. From your reading and note-making, you will begin to find that different authors make similar or contradictory points (**Chs 5, 6, 11** and **12**). As you begin to identify the different schools of thought or approaches to an issue, you should begin to cross-reference your notes so that you can group authors who hold the same or similar viewpoints

Brainstorming techniques

To create an effective concept 'map', use a single sheet of A4 in the landscape position. This gives more space for lateral thinking and creativity. It also leaves more space for additions to be made at later stages. **Figure A2.5** illustrates a model map.

- consider whether any themes or recurrent issues are evident. It might be useful to 'colour code' all the items that are related, using a different colour of highlighter for each category or theme
- use these key themes in the context of the instruction, topic, aspect(s) and restriction(s) to decide how you will describe, analyse and argue within your essay.

ADOPTING A STRUCTURAL APPROACH TO PLANNING YOUR WRITING

People and their thought processes are different and so individual approaches to planning an outline response to a writing assignment will vary. For some people, this can be a highly detailed process; for others, it may be a minimal exercise. Too much detail in a plan can be restricting, while too little can fail to provide enough direction. Therefore, a reasonably detailed plan should give some guidance, while leaving you the flexibility to alter the finer elements as you write.

The reporter's questions

Sometimes it is difficult to distinguish the important from the unimportant, the relevant from the irrelevant. A well-tried strategy, applicable in many subjects, is to ask yourself the questions that trainee journalists are advised to use:

- **Who**? Who is involved in relation to this topic? For example, which people or organisations?
- **What**? What are the problems/issues involved?
- **When?** What is the time-frame to be considered?
- **Where?** Where did it occur?
- **Why?** What reasons are relevant to this issue/topic?
- **How?** How has this situation been reached?

✔ Thinking and writing and thinking

Even the best of plans can alter as you begin to write. Thinking inspires writing but writing, in turn, stimulates further thinking. This can mean that, as you write your plan and then write following your plan, your ideas may change, new ideas may emerge and even the thrust of your argument might shift in direction. Being aware that this can happen is significant because your writing may take longer, may need a major rethink or revision of what you have written already. In terms of time management, it is important to write in some 'extra time for the unexpected' into your timetable so that you do have time to reshape your writing, if necessary. The end-product will, in all probability, result in a much better piece of writing.

Your potential to achieve better marks will be improved if your writing follows a sequence of sound, well-structured logic and argument. However, at this stage, you may yet have to evolve your response to the task you have been set. Using the framework described in **Chapter 9** can help you to sort out ideas and begin to see the various emergent relationships of fact, evidence, theory and hypothesis and the threads of logic.

Table 15.1 shows eight model frameworks that help set out the logic of analysis and argument. Using one of these approaches, a situation can be presented coherently. Note that, sometimes, it may be necessary to incorporate one of these models within another. For example, within the common denominator approach, it may be necessary to include some chronological description within the discussion.

Examples of each of these eight approaches are given below.

1 Chronological

An example of the chronological approach would be describing a developmental process, such as outlining the historical development of the European Union. This kind of writing is likely to be entirely descriptive.

Table 15.1 The eight most common structural approaches for written assignments

Structural approach	Characteristics
1 Chronological	Description of a process or sequence
2 Classification	Categorising objects or ideas
3 Common denominator	Identification of common characteristics or themes
4 Phased	Identification of short-/medium-/long-term aspects
5 Analytical	Examination of an issue in depth e.g.: situation – problem – solution – evaluation – recommendation
6 Thematic	Comment on a theme in each aspect
7 Cause and effect	Analysis of events or processes linking cause(s) with corresponding effect(s)
8 Comparative/contrastive	Discussion of similarities and differences (often within a theme or themes)

2 Classification

This approach could be used to discuss the topic of transport by subdividing your text into land, sea and air modes of travel. Each of these could be further divided into commercial, military and personal modes of transport. These categories could be further sub-divided on the basis of how they are powered. Such classifications are, to some extent, subjective, but the approach provides a means of describing each category at each level in a way that allows some contrast.

This approach is particularly useful in scientific disciplines. The rationale also is sympathetic to the approach of starting from broad generalisation to the more specific (Ch 9).

3 Common denominator

An example of this approach might be used in response to the following assignment: 'Account for the levels of high infant mortality in developing countries'. This suggests a common denominator of deficiency or lack. This topic could therefore be approached under the headings:

- Lack of primary health care
- Lack of health education
- Lack of literacy.

4 Phased

An example of adopting a sequential approach to a topic might be in answer to a task that instructs: 'Discuss the impact of water shortage on flora and fauna along river banks'.

- Short-term factors might be that drying out of the river bed occurs and annual plants fail to thrive.
- Medium-term factors might include damage to oxygenating plant life and reduction of wild-life numbers.
- Long-term factors might include the effect on the water table and falling numbers of certain amphibious species.

5 Analytical

This approach might be used to examine complex issues. An example of an assignment that you could tackle in this way might be: 'Evaluate potential solutions to the problem of identity theft'. You could perhaps adopt the following plan:

- define identity theft, and possibly give an example;
- explain why identity theft is difficult to control;
- outline legal and practical solutions to preventing identify theft;
- weigh up the advantages and disadvantages of each;
- state which solution(s) you would favour and why.

 Adopting an analytical approach

The analytical approach is particularly helpful in the construction of essays, reports, projects and case studies. It is also useful whenever you feel that you cannot identify themes or trends. This approach helps you to 'deconstruct' or 'unpack' the topic and involves five elements:

- **Situation**: describe the context and brief history
- **Problem**: describe or define the problem
- **Solution**: describe and explain the possible solution(s)
- **Evaluation**: identify the positive and negative features for each solution by giving evidence/reasons to support your viewpoint
- **Recommendation**: identify the best option in your opinion, giving the basis of your reasoning for this. This element is optional, as it may not always be a requirement of your task.

6 Thematic

This approach is similar to the phased approach, but in this case themes are the identifying characteristics. Precise details would depend on the nature of the question, but possible examples could be:

- social, economic or political factors;
- age, income and health considerations;
- gas, electricity, oil, water and wind power and their relative merits.

7 Comparative/contrastive

This is a derivative of the themed approach For example, consider a task that instructs 'Discuss the arguments for and against the introduction of car-free city centres'. You might approach this by creating a grid, similar to **Figure 2.6**, which notes positive and negative aspects for the major stakeholders.

Potential methods using this approach are:

- **Method 1**

  Introductory statement on the topic

  Discuss A points (A1 + A2 + A3 + A4 + A5)

  Discuss B points (B1 + B2 + B3 + B4 + B5)

  Concluding statement on the merits and demerits of A and B

- **Method 2**

  Introductory statement on the topic

  Discuss point A1 then counter point B1

  Discuss point A2 then counter point B2

  Discuss point A3 then counter point B3

  Discuss point A4 then counter point B4

  Discuss point A5 then counter point B5

  Concluding statement on the merits and demerits of A and B.

8 Cause and effect

This has similarities to the phased approach. Causal relationships – sometimes termed cause → effect, sometimes reason → result – can be explained using a themed approach of short-medium-long effects as shown here. At other times, the time dimension is less relevant. For example, topics in this category do not always prompt this sort of response directly by asking for 'results' or consequences of an event; it could be used to respond to a task such as: 'Explain the influences of poverty on poor diet in modern urban society'.

EXPANDING YOUR OUTLINE

Once you have decided the kind of approach required to cover your written assignment, then you can formulate this as the main body of your essay and frame an introduction and conclusion that will 'top and tail' your writing. In this way you can expand the outline plan based on the introduction – main body – conclusion model that follows the framework for academic writing examined in **Chapter 9**.

At this stage in your planning, you should check that the points you plan for your introduction correspond broadly to the points listed for your conclusion, remembering that you should not introduce new material in your conclusion.

Which method of presentation of comparative/ contrastive structures is better?

Each method of structuring the points has advantages and disadvantages, according to the context of the assignment. For example, in an exam it might be risky to embark on Method 1 in case you run out of time and never reach the discussion of column B. In this instance, Method 2 would enable a balanced answer. In coursework rather than an exam, Method 2 has the advantage that it allows for more measured consideration of the corresponding points at the same stage. For long and complex topics where there are many points of comparison/ contrast, the second method offers greater integration of each aspect under consideration. Method 1 has the advantage that it allows for a continuous appraisal of allied aspects (in this case the positive and then negative aspects). This can suit some topics where it is important to establish the case in its entirety before considering counter-points.

Try 'negating' the wording. Sometimes balance is difficult to achieve in academic tasks. People can tend to focus on only one aspect of an issue. Sometimes it is helpful to turn the task around by rewording it in a negative format. For example, 'How has prison become too easy a punishment?' becomes 'How has prison not become too easy a punishment?' The points raised by the second question may throw up different dimensions and so expand your plan and introduce balance into your answer.

Start with the main body. Logical progression through the finished writing will take the reader from introduction to main body and then to the conclusion (**Ch 9**). However, in terms of actually writing the text, although you might know roughly how your text will be presented, how it pans out in the final format may be different from initial expectations or your plan. Thus, it is better to start working from the structure of the main body, and then follow through on the conclusion before you construct the introduction.

Explain your approach. Your reader will benefit from understanding how you intend to tackle the issue in your text. Your reader should learn at an early point in our writing, the route that you intend to follow. In most cases, this would be in your introduction.

 **And now ...**

15.1 Compare textual patterns. Choose a chapter in a basic textbook and analyse the structural approach the author has taken. Identify the proportion of space allocated to 'scene setting' using description and to the analyse/argument/evaluation components of the text.

15.2 Identify response types. Read over some of the assignment titles you have been set. Try to identify which of the approaches given in this chapter might best 'fit' each task.

15.3 Practise converting questions into instructions. If past exam papers/coursework exercises include tasks framed as questions, try converting them to instruction formats and decide which type they fit into within the 'do-describe-analyse-argue' classification (**Ch 8**).

16

WRITING A FIRST DRAFT

How to shape your text using sentences and paragraphs effectively

Moving from the plan to writing the text requires creativity, patience and perseverance. The first draft is a document that puts the ideas on the plan into words but the process of perfecting these words requires critical thinking, appropriate use and citation of the work of others alongside an understanding of how language works at sentence and paragraph levels.

KEY TOPICS

→ How sentences work

→ How paragraphs work

→ Using knowledge of text structure in writing

→ Monitoring citations and compiling the reference list

KEY UNIVERSITY TERMS

Clause   Subject   Subordinate clause   Verb

Writers tackle academic writing differently. Some people can work from a skeletal plan comprising only a few headings while others prefer to work from a detailed plan. For the less experienced, adopting the detailed plan is probably the choice that leads to a more structured and logical text. As explained in **Chapters 9** and **15**, the plan can be formulated to follow the principles of the 'introduction-main body-conclusion' model integrating one of the structural approaches that is most suited to your topic.

This chapter explains further **Step 8** in the writing process introduced in **Chapter 8** by considering the practical aspects of preparing to write the first draft. Initially, this means examining aspects of the structure of the elements of text, namely:

- how sentences and paragraphs work
- how knowledge of text structure contributes to shaping writing.

Lack of understanding in these areas can introduce barriers to writing. To overcome such barriers, it is often helpful to begin the actual writing with a section of the text that is descriptive – for example, you might outline the context of the problem that you are addressing. Since describing is often perceived as an 'easier' writing activity, this can encourage an episode of fluent writing that can inspire your writing on more complex aspects.

Some people can find it difficult to form their ideas into coherent text and will work on a single sentence for a long time. Knowing how sentences are constructed will help to overcome this barrier.

HOW SENTENCES WORK

What is a sentence? A sentence must have a verb, that is, a 'doing' word (**Appendix 9**). Each of the following is a sentence (verb in bold):

Help!

Students **work** in the holidays.

Universities **provide** tuition in a wide range of subjects.

Simple sentences

These have at least a *subject* (the person or thing doing the action) and a **verb**, sometimes followed by a phrase of other information. Together these make sense as a unit. For example:

Criminal Law **differs** from Civil Law.

Plants **require** sunlight and water.

Divalent ions **carry** two charges.

Compound sentences

These are two simple sentences joined by **and** or **but**. There will be two verbs in this combined sentence. For example:

The protocols for these determinations **are** lengthy (typically over 7 hours) **and** they **require** careful sample preparation.

Scots Law and English Law **are** fundamentally different, **but** they **are** similar in some areas.

'Dangling phrases'

Dangling phrases do not make sentences, for example:

Bringing the debate to an end.

Having been at war for 100 years.

Gum trees **being** susceptible to termite infestation.

The bold words denote dangling phrases. They do contain verbs, but these are only in participle form (present participles, **Appendix 9**) and not fully formed verbs. Such phrases often make little sense. They are isolated from other words that provide a context or relationship. The use of such dangling phrases is common in student essays.

Here is a correct version of a sentence that uses a participle phrase. In this case, the participle phrase needs to relate to the subject of the main clause (both shown in bold):

The **countries** of Europe, **having been at war for 100 years**, were financially exhausted.

Complex sentences

These sentences consist of a main clause with additional subordinate clauses. A clause is a unit of meaning built round a verb. There are two categories of clause: principal (sometimes called independent or main clause, which is like a simple sentence) and subordinate clauses.

The subordinate clause contains a verb, but would not make sense if it were to stand alone. It does the work of an adjective, adverb or noun.

The following are examples of subordinate clauses (shown in bold):

Gait analysis gives insights into the walking difficulties **that are experienced by people with cerebral palsy**.

Social work legislation protects the rights of the elderly **when they are no longer able to cope independently**.

Although Britain is regarded as a democracy, it has no written constitution **that can be cited as the basis of Constitutional Law**.

Complex sentences can be quite long and can contain more than one subordinate clause. Varying the length of your sentences enlivens your text and helps to keep your reader's interest. However, shorter sentences containing a single idea can often have a stronger impact than longer complex sentences. If you want to balance two ideas, then compound sentences are best.

Models for academic writing: what to avoid

Newspaper journalism and layout favours paragraphs of single sentences, but these are not good models for academic writing. Similarly, adopting a flowery or pompous style is not appropriate to academic writing. See **Chapter 10** for further tips.

HOW PARAGRAPHS WORK

What is a paragraph? A paragraph is a unit of text usually comprising several sentences. It has a topic that is outlined in the first sentence; the topic is developed further within the paragraph; and the paragraph concludes with a sentence that terminates that topic or, possibly, acts as a link to the topic of the following paragraph.

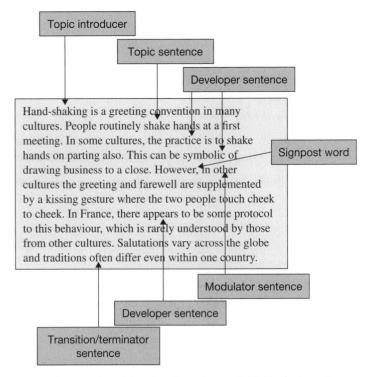

Figure 16.1 How sentences make up a paragraph. Part of a text on Anthropology, showing how different types of sentences are used to construct a paragraph.

Paragraph structure

The building blocks of paragraphs are sentences, each performing a particular role: as detailed in Table 16.1, and seen in action within the example shown in Figure 16.1. This example is a very straightforward listing paragraph.

Table 16.2 gives examples of signpost, or linking, words that you can use to join the component sentences within a paragraph so that your text flows smoothly and Table 16.3 provides a range of different paragraph models.

If the building blocks of paragraphs are sentences, then paragraphs themselves are the building blocks of text. Each paragraph performs a particular role within the structure of the text. Thus, paragraphs can describe (position, time, process, appearance), define, classify, give examples, generalise, list, relate cause and effect, as well as compare and contrast. The examples of paragraph formats shown in Table 16.3 can be used to construct extended written text. The example in Figure 16.2 shows mechanisms of generating paragraph flow within a piece of text.

Table 16.1 Some types of sentences that are used to make up a paragraph

Type of sentence	Role in the paragraph
Topic introducer sentence	Introduces the overall topic of the text (generally in the very first paragraph)
Topic sentence	Introduces a paragraph by identifying the topic of that paragraph
Developer sentence	Expands the topic by giving additional information
Modulator sentence	Acts as linking sentence and is often introduced by a signpost word moving to another aspect of the topic within the same paragraph
Terminator sentence	Concludes the discussion of a topic within a paragraph, but can also be used as a **transition sentence** where it provides a link to the topic of the next paragraph

Table 16.2 Signpost words in text. This table provides examples of words and phrases that can be used to improve the flow of your writing.

Type of link intended	Examples of signpost words
Addition	additionally; furthermore; in addition; moreover
Cause/reason	as a result of; because (mid-sentence)
Comparison	compared with; in the same way; in comparison with; likewise
Condition	if; on condition that; providing that; unless
Contrast	although; by contrast; conversely; despite; however; nevertheless; yet
Effect/result	as a result; hence; therefore; thus
Exemplification	for example; for instance; particularly; such as; thus
Reformulation	in other words; rather; to paraphrase
Summary	finally; hence; in all; in conclusion; in short; in summary
Time sequence	after; at first; at last; before; eventually; subsequently
Transition	as far as … is concerned; as for; to turn to

Table 16.3 Paragraph models. The construction of paragraph types is modelled under each heading. The numbers of intermediate sentences of each type is arbitrary – you could use more or fewer according to the need or context.

Describing: appearance/position	Describing: time sequence
• Topic introducer • Developer 1 • Developer 2 • Developer 3 • Terminator sentence Descriptive sequence examples: top to bottom; left to right; centre to perimeter	Either: • Event 1 • Event 2 • Event 3 Or: • By date order
Describing: process – how it works	**Defining**
• Topic introducer • Developer 1 • Developer 2 … • Modulator • Developer 1 • Developer 2 … • Topic sentence	• Topic sentence • Example 1 • Example 2 • Example 3 • Terminator sentence Note: Don't use a different form of the word being defined in order to define it

Table 16.3 continued

Classifying	Generalising
• Topic sentence • Example 1 • Example 2 ... • Terminator sentence identifying category	• Developer 1 • Developer 2 ... • Topic sentence; generalisation Or: • Generalisation • Developer 1 • Developer 2 ... • Restatement sentence
Giving examples	**Listing**
• Topic sentence • Example 1 • Example 2 ... • Restatement sentence or terminator sentence	• Topic sentence • Developer sentence • Modulator sentence • Developer sentence • Terminator sentence
Relating cause and effect: method 1	**Relating cause and effect: method 2**
• Topic introducer • Topic sentence • Developer 1 • Developer 2 • Modulator • Developer 3 • Developer 4 • Terminator/restatement sentence	• Topic introducer • Topic sentence • Developer 1 Theme A • Developer 2 Theme A • Modulator (transfer to B) • Developer 1 Theme B • Developer 2 Theme B • Terminator/restatement sentence
Comparing	**Contrasting**
• Topic introducer • Topic sentence • Developer 1 Theme A • Developer 2 Theme A ... • Modulator (transfer to B) • Developer 1 Theme B • Developer 2 Theme B ... • Restatement sentence	• Topic introducer • Topic sentence • Developer 1 Theme A • Developer 1 Theme B • Developer 2 Theme A • Developer 2 Theme B ... • Terminator • Restatement sentence

Traffic congestion is problematic in the urban environment. Existing infrastructure of road and public transport links has proved to be inadequate. Gridlock has become a frequent occurrence within cities and solutions need to be found.	Topic introducer; generalising paragraph
The need to respond to daily commuter migrations has caused much debate. Analysis of travel patterns has shown that commuters prefer the convenience of personal transport over using public transport, which they claim to be inefficient, costly and even dangerous. **Conversely**, planners and politicians see this attitude as selfish and the single most significant contributory factor to inner-city congestion and pollution.	Topic developer; contrasting paragraph 1
Green activists consider that all forms of fossil-fuelled transport are environmentally unfriendly, but concede that the lesser of the evils is the use of public transport. **However**, ideally their fundamental view is to encourage the creation of cycle lanes and urban pathways that will entice people into cycling or walking to work.	Topic developer; contrasting paragraph 2
The commuter, **by contrast**, has to consider cost, travel time and relative distance. This is not simply a case of convenience. Many people choose to improve their quality of life by living outside the urban areas, thus the distances that people are prepared to travel increase in proportion to the cheaper cost of housing in non-metropolitan areas. For many, public transport is simply not a viable option and car-sharing is another way of achieving convenience while reducing travel time and cost.	Topic developer; contrasting paragraph 3

Figure 16.2 **How paragraphs make up a piece of text.** Part of an essay on town planning, showing how different paragraphs have been used to construct a flowing piece of text. Note how the emboldened signpost words (Table 16.2) have been used.

As an academic writer you will develop skills in constructing these different types of paragraph and in sequencing them to create logically organised text that helps the reader to understand your line of reasoning. This is a good reason for planning your writing carefully (**Ch 15**). In addition, you also need to be aware that both sentences and paragraphs can be ordered in different ways to establish the structure of the discussion in your text, that is, deductively or inductively.

1 **Inductive model of text structure**: the writer presents the supporting information and concludes with the main point

2 **Deductive model of text structure**: the writer moves from the key idea and follows it with supporting information or evidence.

These models may be deployed according to discipline style or simply to mix up the approaches used in your writing.

Inductive and deductive logic in writing

The sequences of statements shown here could represent the themes of sentences within a paragraph.

Inductive model – moving from examples to general principle(s)

1 Lecturer A wears out-of-date clothes from the 1980s
2 Lecturer B wears out-of-date clothes from the 1990s
3 Lecturer C wears out-of-date clothes from the 2000s
4 Therefore, all lecturers wear out-of-date clothes of one type or another

Deductive model – moving from general principle(s) to particular instances

1 All lecturers wear out-of-date clothes of one type or another
2 Person D is a lecturer
3 Therefore, Person D will wear out-of-date clothes

USING KNOWLEDGE OF TEXT STRUCTURE IN WRITING

Knowing some of the finer points about sentence structure and the roles that they play within paragraphs gives you the ability to be more critical of what you write. Typical weaknesses lie in:

- **Non-sequential sentences** – where the order of the sentences does not follow a logical sequence such as those described in **Chapter 5** and Table 16.3.

- **Overlong sentences** – these may be difficult for the reader to understand. As a rough guide sentences more than 3 lines of text (or 40 words) need to be revisited for editing or dividing into shorter sentences. Consider:

    Using plagiarism detection software is potentially a costly business since it requires the purchase of expensive software licenses but it can mean that there is less chance of a student submitting material that has been drawn from online sources and using these to supplement their own writing or, in some cases, even submit in its entirety as their own work. [60 words]

By using shorter sentences, it is possible to create text that is more easily read and that provides the information in shorter chunks that are easier to assimilate:

Using plagiarism detection software is potentially a costly business, since expensive software licenses have to be purchased. Nevertheless, its use can mean that there is less chance of a student submitting material that has been drawn from online sources. For example, some students use downloaded material to supplement their own writing or, in some cases, even submit in its entirety as their own work. [64 words over three sentences]

Clearly the group of sentences sends three clear pieces of information succinctly compared to the long-winded single sentence in the first example.

- **Non-sentences** – a group of words or a short phrase that lacks grammatical structure. For example, a subject and verb to create the most basic of simple sentences may be lacking: 'But to cross the river' is not a sentence and might only make sense after the sentence 'There was no other option.' Another type of non-sentence occurs where the writer has composed a 'dangling' participial phrase (usually introduced by a word ending in '-ing') that fails to relate grammatically to the preceding or following text. This is a common flaw. An example of this kind of 'dangler' might be: 'Pushing the boundaries of knowledge.' As a sequence of words, this has no context in which to place the sense of the phrase. However, if followed by 'has given academics recognition in society.', then context and grammatical form are achieved. Note that in speech, people often use half-sentences or dangling phrases and these work well enough where facial and other cues provide a context; in written work, these are simply wrong.

- **Non-sensical sentences** – where the words used or their order makes the sentence meaningless or where some word or words have been omitted so that, again, the result is meaningless or at best ambiguous.

Here is an authentic example:

Referral letters are screened and allocated to see the most appropriate member of the medical team to deal with your problem.

In each of these instances, reading your work aloud will allow your ears to pick up errors of logic or grammar that your eyes have missed.

By going back to your plan and identifying each point that you wish to make, you can group these according to their relationships; these groupings might represent paragraphs. You then create a topic sentence that would introduce these points/paragraphs. Writing subsequent developer and modulator sentences (Figure 16.1) will allow you to produce a draft paragraph. You can then review the paragraph to ensure that it avoids any errors such as those listed previously. Table 16.4 gives some further tips about how 'playing with text' can improve your writing.

MONITORING CITATIONS AND COMPILING THE REFERENCE LIST

The use of citations to support your writing was explained in detail in **Chapter 12** as **Step 9** in the 12-step process of writing. Citations are important in avoiding plagiarism.

As noted, as your text begins to take shape, you will introduce the work of others to reflect your understanding and analysis of your topic. Using direct quotation (if appropriate), or the information-prominent or author-prominent formats explained in **Chapter 12**, you will be able to provide the facts, information, concepts, theories or evidence, with the corresponding citation to support your scrutiny of the topic.

At this draft stage, as suggested in **Chapter 12**, alongside creating the first draft of **Step 8**, it will save time and effort, if you begin **Step 9** of the writing process, by constructing your list of references as you write. This ensures that no reference is forgotten and takes the chore out of typing up a tediously lengthy reference list at the end of your writing when time might be tight and your energy low.

PRACTICAL TIPS FOR USING SENTENCES AND PARAGRAPHS EFFECTIVELY

How long is a sentence? This is a 'how long is a piece of string?' type of question. A sentence can be long or short. There are two tests for good sentence structure. First, simply read it out aloud. Your ear will usually detect inconsistencies or information overload. Second, if you feel a need to take a breath in mid-sentence, then a comma is probably needed, or even a full stop followed by a new sentence.

Table 16.4 Examples of how 'playing with language' can improve your writing. Writing can often be improved by rearranging the order of words or phrases, by choosing more suitable words or by separating out ideas into independent elements. Examples A–C below illustrate possible techniques that you might adopt.

A. Heads and tails

Sometimes a sentence works better if you experiment by shifting elements around within it. A phrase or clause that is at the tail end of the sentence might be more powerful, and emphasise your meaning more strongly, if it is positioned at the head of the sentence. For example:

Version A1: *The practical application of 'duty to disclose' in relation to the onset of multiple sclerosis was deliberately entrusted to the discretion of the medical profession **because it was seen as impossible to define in policy**.*

could become

Version A2: *Since it was considered impossible to define 'duty to disclose' in policy in relation to the onset of multiple sclerosis, the practical application was deliberately entrusted to the medical profession.*

Both instances have validity. However, as a writer, you might wish to place the emphasis on the reason for the failure to define a policy. In that case, Version A2 would be better. However, if you felt the emphasis should rest with the role of the medical profession, then Version A1 would be better. This shows the importance of considering your intention as you construct and review your writing, and it emphasises how important applying logic is to the whole process.

B. Better word, clearer meaning

Academic writing should, by definition, be both precise and concise. However, sometimes in the process of writing the need to record the ideas overtakes the accuracy and clarity that might be desirable. Consequently, take time to review your work to identify ways in which you can use words more appropriately to achieve clarity. For example:

Version B1: *The practical application of 'duty to disclose' in relation to the onset of multiple sclerosis was deliberately entrusted to **the decision-making process operating** in the medical profession because it was seen as impossible to define in policy.*

could become

Version B2: *The practical application of 'duty to disclose' in relation to the onset of multiple sclerosis was deliberately entrusted to the **discretion** of the medical profession because it was seen as impossible to define in policy.*

Not only is Version B2 clearer than Version B1, but it expresses more aptly the leeway that the situation implies.

C. Long and short sentences

Sometimes it is better to split an overly long or complex sentence. For example:

Version C1: *The practical application of 'duty to disclose' in relation to the onset of multiple sclerosis was deliberately entrusted to the discretion of the medical profession **because it was seen as impossible to define in policy**.*

could become

Version C2: *The practical application of 'duty to disclose' in relation to the onset of multiple sclerosis was deliberately entrusted to the discretion of the medical profession. **This decision was reached because it was seen as impossible to define in policy**.*

Version C1 places the reason as a tag on the end of the main clause, whereas Version C2 emphasises the reason by stating it as a separate sentence.

How long is a paragraph? The length of a paragraph depends on the content, but generally extra-long paragraphs will have some topic shift within them. If you find that your paragraph seems disproportionately long, then, again, read it aloud and listen for a 'natural' break point. This is probably a good place to start a new paragraph.

Use signpost words. These words are used to assist your reader by moving them through the logic of your text, for example, in modulator sentences. Some words are most frequently used at the beginning of sentences: for example, however, moreover, furthermore, nevertheless. These are followed by a comma and then the point you wish to make.

(GO) And now ...

16.1 Take tips from the professionals. Select a short section from a textbook. Analyse a couple of paragraphs, looking, in particular, for the introducers, developers, modulators (and signpost words) and transition/terminator sentences. Now select text from a piece of your own writing and do the same thing. How balanced is the paragraph structure? Have you overused or underused signpost words?

16.2 Assess your own writing for clarity of meaning. Continuing with your own text, check for clarity and conciseness. Have you used any dangling phrases (non-sentences)? Have you used simple or compound (joined by 'and' or 'but') sentences too often? Are your sentences perhaps too complex? Are there too many subordinate clauses? Could some overlong sentences be modified to become simpler?

16.3 Refer to Appendix 7 on punctuation. There are tips on how to use commas, colons and semicolons in extended writing. These punctuation marks are important in breaking up ideas in text into paragraphs and sentences. With this information beside you, look critically at your own writing. Try to spot places where it might be helpful to your reader if you modified the punctuation to make your sentences and paragraphs clearer and unambiguous. Again, reading aloud will help you identify where punctuation is incorrect or is missing.

17

REVIEWING, EDITING AND PROOF-READING YOUR WRITING

How to make sure your writing is concise and correct

Checking your own writing is essential if you want to produce work of the highest quality. These editing skills will allow you to improve the sense, grammar and syntax of your written assignments so that the content of your work is presented to your reader as accessible and intelligible.

KEY UNIVERSITY TOPICS

→ Your role as reviewer, editor and proof-reader

→ The value of reviewing, editing and proof-reading

KEY UNIVERSITY TERMS

Annotate   Syntax   Typo   *vice versa*

Following the 12-step writing process (**Table 1.1**), this chapter continues with **Step 10**, that is, the stage at which reviewing, editing and proof-reading take place (**Chapters 13** and **14**). This is a critical step and one that is often missed out by students who are rushing to meet their deadline. As suggested in **Chapter 8**, if you have been efficient in creating and keeping to your timetable, you should have time to complete this tenth step.

YOUR ROLE AS REVIEWER, EDITOR AND PROOF-READER

By this stage, you will have invested a considerable time and effort into producing your text. Therefore, it takes real discipline to 'stand back' from your work and appraise it critically as a reviewer, editor and proof-reader. The process involves checking for:

- content, relevance and sense
- clarity, style and coherence
- flaws in layout and grammar
- consistency in use of terminology, spelling of specialist terms
- presentational features.

Check that all the 'secretarial' aspects are in place. Neat presentation, punctuation and spelling all help your reader to access the information, ideas and argument of your writing. While this may not gain you marks, it will ensure that you do not lose marks, even indirectly, by making the marker struggle to 'decode' your work.

Clearly, there are many aspects to cover, and some degree of overlap in different parts of the process. Some people prefer to go through their text in one sweep, amending any flaws as they go; others, in particular professional writers, take a staged approach, reading through their text several times looking at a different facet each time.

Definitions

Reviewing: appraising critically; that is, examining an essay or assignment to ensure that it meets the requirements and objectives of the task and that the overall sense is conveyed well.

Editing: revising and correcting later drafts of an essay or assignment, to arrive at a final version. Usually, this involves the smaller rather than the larger details: punctuation, spelling, grammar and layout.

Proof-reading: checking a printed copy for errors of any sort.

Table 17.1 provides a quick checklist of key aspects to consider under each of these themes. This has been designed for photocopying so that you can, if you wish, use it as a checklist each time you complete a piece of work. Table 17.2 gives some helpful strategies you can adopt when going through the editing process.

Professional proof-readers have developed a system of symbols to speed up the editing and proof-reading process. You may wish to adopt some of these yourself, and you are certainly likely to see some of them, and other 'informal' marks, on work returned by tutors. Table 17.3 illustrates some of the more commonly used symbols.

Table 17.1 Quick editing and proof-reading checklist. Each heading could represent a 'sweep' of your text, checking for the aspects shown. The text is assumed to be a piece of writing produced for assessment.

Content and relevance
❏ The intent of the instruction word has been followed
❏ The question or task has been completed, that is, you have answered all sections or completed the required numbers of tasks
❏ The structure is appropriate
❏ The text shows objectivity
❏ The examples are relevant
❏ All sources are correctly cited
❏ The facts presented are accurate

Clarity, style and coherence
❏ The rationale of your approach to the topic will be clear to the reader
❏ What you wrote is what you meant to write
❏ The text is fluent, with appropriate use of signpost words
❏ Any informal language has been removed
❏ The style is academic and appropriate for the task
❏ The content and style of each section is consistent
❏ The tense used in each section is suited to the time frame of your text
❏ The length of the text sections are balanced appropriately

Grammatical correctness
❏ All sentences are complete
❏ All sentences make sense
❏ Paragraphs have been correctly used
❏ Suggestions made by grammar checker have been accepted/rejected
❏ Text has been checked against your own checklist of recurrent errors
❏ Text is consistent in adopting either British or American English

Spelling and punctuation
❏ Any blatant 'typos' have been corrected by reading for meaning
❏ Text has been spellchecked or read through carefully for spelling
❏ A check has been made for spelling of subject-specific and foreign words
❏ Punctuation has been checked, if possible, by reading aloud
❏ Proper names are correctly capitalised
❏ Overlong sentences have been divided

Presentation
❏ If no word-count target is given, the overall length will depend on the amount of time you were given to complete the task. Ask your tutor, if you're uncertain
❏ The text length meets the word-count target – neither too short nor too long
❏ Overall neatness checked
❏ The cover-sheet details and presentation aspects are as required
❏ The bibliography/reference list is correctly formatted according to the recommended style
❏ Page numbers have been included (in position stipulated, if given)
❏ The figures and tables are in appropriate format

Table 17.2 Editing strategies – quick reference. The reviewing/editing/ proof-reading process can be done in a single 'sweep'. As you become more experienced, you will become adept at doing this. However, initially, it might help you to focus on each of these three broad aspects in a separate 'sweep' of the text. Note that the first two sections develop aspects considered in Table 17.1. **Chapter 13** addresses presentational issues in detail.

Content and relevance; clarity, style and coherence
• Work on a hard copy using editing symbols to correct errors (Table 17.3)
• Read text aloud – your ears will help you to identify errors that your eyes have missed
• Revisit the task or question. Check your interpretation against the task as set
• Identify that the aims you set out in your introduction have been met
• Read objectively and assess whether the text makes sense. Look for inconsistencies in argument
• Check that all your facts are correct
• Insert additional or overlooked evidence that strengthens the whole
• Remove anything that is not relevant or alter the text so that it is clear and unambiguous. Reducing text by 10–25 per cent can improve quality considerably
• Critically assess your material to ensure that you have attributed ideas to the sources, that is, check that you have not committed plagiarism
• Remodel any expressions that are too informal for academic contexts
• Eliminate gendered or discriminatory language

Grammatical correctness, spelling and punctuation
• Check titles and subtitles are appropriate to the style of the work and stand out by using bold or underlining (not both)
• Consider whether the different parts link together well – if not, introduce signpost words to guide the reader through the text (Table 16.2)
• Check for fluency in sentence and paragraph structure – remodel as required
• Check sentence length – remodel to shorter or longer sentences. Sometimes shorter sentences are more effective than longer ones
• Ensure that you have been consistent in spelling conventions, for example, following British English rather than American English spelling or *vice versa*
• Spelling errors – use the spellchecker but be prepared to double-check in a standard dictionary if you are in doubt or cannot find a spelling within the spellchecker facility
• Check punctuation, especially to avoid cumbersome constructions – divide or restructure sentence(s); consider whether active or passive is more suitable. Consider using vocabulary that might convey your point more eloquently
• Check for use of 'absolute' terms to ensure that you maintain objectivity

Table 17.2 continued

Presentation
• Check that you have made good use of white space, that is, not crammed the text into too tight a space, and that your text is neat and legible with minimum 1.5 line spacing if no recommendation is made otherwise
• If your text is word-processed, check that you have followed standard typing conventions. Follow any 'house style' rules stipulated by your department
• Check that you have included a reference list, consistently following a recognised method, and that all citations in the text are matched by an entry in the reference list and *vice versa*
• Ensure all pages are numbered and are stapled or clipped, and, if appropriate, ensure that the cover page is included
• Check that your name, matriculation number and course number are included. You may wish to add this information as a footer that appears on each page
• Ensure question number and title are included
• Check that labelling of diagrams, charts and other visual material is in sequence and consistently presented
• Ensure that supporting material is added in sequence as appendices, footnotes, endnotes or a glossary, as applicable

 Technical notes

The word processor has made the reviewing and editing task much easier. Here are some tips for using this software effectively.

■ Use the word-count facility to check on length.

■ Use the 'View' facility to check page breaks and general layout before you print out.

■ Use the facilities within the 'Format' or 'Page layout' menu to control presentational aspects like paragraph spacing, tabs for indents and styles for bulleted and numbered lists.

■ Use the spell– and grammar-checkers to guide you, but do not rely on them 100 per cent as they are fallible.

■ Sometimes the grammar checker will show that you have used the passive voice. This is often a standard academic usage and, therefore, is not an error.

■ Sometimes staff add comments to students' work using 'Track Changes' on the Microsoft Word software. Depending on the version you are using, feedback information can usually be accepted or rejected by right-clicking on the word or punctuation point that has been marked for alteration.

Table 17.3 Common proof-reading symbols. University lecturers and tutors use a variety of symbols on students' assignments to indicate errors, corrections or suggestions. These can apply to punctuation, spelling, presentation or grammar. The symbols provide a kind of 'shorthand' that acts as a code to help you see how you might be able to amend your text so that it reads correctly and fluently. In this table some of the more commonly used correction marks are shown alongside their meanings. The sample text shows how these symbols may be used either in the text or the margin to indicate where a change is recommended.

Correction mark	Meaning	Example
⌐ (np)	(new) paragraph	*Text* *margin*
≢	change CAPITALS to small letters (lower case)	The correction marks that tutors
∿	change into **bold** type	use in students' texts are generally ⅄
≡	change into CAPITALS	made to help identify where there
◡	close up (delete space)	have been errors of spelling or ʎe/ʎg
/ or ⁊ or ⊢	delete	punctuation. They can often (STET)
ʎ	insert a word or letter	indicate where there is lack of
⅄	insert space	paragraphing or grammatical
.... or (STET)	leave unchanged	accuracy. If you find that work is (np)
Insert punctuation symbol in a circle (P)	punctuation	returned to you with such marks correction, then it is ⊔⊓ worthwhile spending some time
plag.	plagiarism	analysing the common errors as ⁊ well as the comments, because this
⟶	run on (no new paragraph)	will help you to improve the quality of presentation and content
Sp.	spelling	of your work this reviewing can ⊙/≡
⊔⊓	transpose text	have a positive effect on your
?	what do you mean?	assessed mark.
??	text does not seem to make sense	
✓	good point/correct	*In the margin, the error symbols are separated by a slash (/) if there is more than one error per line.*
x	error	

THE VALUE OF REVIEWING, EDITING AND PROOF-READING

Although the editing process may seem tedious and more complex than it might have appeared at first, a text revised in this way will be far more likely to receive a favourable reading – and possibly a higher mark – than one that is not reviewed, edited and proofed.

Professional writers – novelists as well as academics – often report that their initial drafts are often much longer than the final version. If you follow their example of writing 'large' and then cutting down the text with intelligent editing, then your text will be crisper. Some of the things that can be easily removed are redundant words ('in order to = 'to') or lengthy expressions ('a lot of' = 'many') which will help to achieve that crispness of expression. At sentence level, you may find that you have written something like:

These changes have caused shortages in almost all commodities in the market that are derived from milk. This means that milk products are in short-supply.

Essentially, these two sentences mean the same and so you could eliminate one of them. Which one you decide to cut might depend on the context; equally, it might depend on your word count. Either way, the resulting, shorter, text will send a clearer message to your reader.

It is the mix of style, content, structure and presentation that will gain you marks, and anything you can do to increase your mark-earning power will be to your advantage. In the longer term, learning how to edit your work properly will help you to develop a skill of critical analysis that will stand you in good stead throughout your career.

The practical tips that follow give more detailed explanation of how to review, edit and proof your work, both for coursework and during exams. These are summarised in the checklist in Table 17.1 and in the quick-reference editing strategies listed in Table 17.2.

Make time for checking. Ensure that you have allowed adequate time for reviewing and proof-reading your writing. You don't want to spoil all your hard work by skimping the final stage. Leave some time between finishing the final draft and to checking the whole text, because you will return to your work with a fresh and possibly more critical eye.

PRACTICAL TIPS FOR REVIEWING, EDITING AND PROOF-READING YOUR WRITING

Make time for checking. When planning the writing of an essay or assignment, ensure that you have allowed adequate time for reviewing and proof-reading. You don't want to spoil all your hard work by skimping on the final stage. Leave some time between finishing the final draft and returning to check the whole text, because you will return to your work with a fresh and possibly more critical eye.

Work from a hard copy. Reading through your work laid out on paper, which is the format in which your marker will probably see it, will help you identify errors and inconsistencies more readily than might be possible on the screen. A paper version is also easier to annotate (although this can also be done using the 'Track Changes' facility on your word processor). A printout also allows you to see the whole work in overview, and focus on the way the text 'flows'. If necessary, spread it out on the desk in front of you.

Map your work to obtain an overview and to use as a revision tool. 'Label' each paragraph with a topic heading and list these in a linear way on a separate paper. This will provide you with a 'snapshot' of your text and will allow you to appraise the order, check against any original plan, and adjust the position of parts as you feel necessary. By applying this method to a marked assignment paper, it could help you to create an overview of the coursework topic that, together with the amendments suggested by your tutor in feedback, may provide you with a convenient and succinct revision tool.

Check for relevance. Ensure that you have written and interpreted the task as set and have not 'made up' another title for the task. Whatever you have written will be judged by the terms of the original question, not by one that you have created.

Check for consistency in the elements of your text. For example, ensure that your introduction and conclusion complement and do not contradict each other.

Stick to your word limits/targets. Remember that too few words can be just as bad as too many. The key point is that your writing must be clear to your reader. Sometimes this means giving a longer explanation; sometimes it means simplifying what you have written. However, at this stage, if you are over the word-count limit, then check for ways in which you can reword the text to eliminate redundant words while maintaining the sense you intended to convey.

Create 'white space'. To help produce a more 'reader-friendly' document that will not deter the marker, try to create 'white space' by:

- leaving space (one 'return' space) between paragraphs
- justifying only on the left side of the page
- leaving space around diagrams, tables and other visual material and
- leaving reasonable spaces between headings, sub-headings and text.

 **And now ...**

17.1 Reflect on past submissions. Look at an essay or assignment that you have already submitted and go through it using the checklist in Table 17.1. Concentrate on two pages and, using a highlighter, mark all flaws, inconsistencies or errors. Look at the overall effect of these errors and reflect on the extent to which this may have lost you marks; then consider how you might allow for more time for the editing/proof-reading phase next time round.

17.2 Practise using the standard proof-reading marks. On the same piece of text, insert the relevant standard proof-reading symbols (Table 17.3) on the text and in the margin. Learning how to use these symbols will help you speed up the proof-reading process when you make the corrections in your final draft.

17.3 Practise condensing a piece of text. This is an acknowledged way of improving your work, though you have to bear in mind any word targets that have been set. Look at your text for irrelevant points, wordy phrases, repetitions and excessive examples; if you can reduce its original length by 10–25 per cent, you will probably find that you have created a much tighter, easier-to-read piece of writing.

DEVELOPING FUTURE ACADEMIC WRITING - HOW TO BUILD ON MARKERS' ADVICE FOR GOOD RESULTS

18

ACTING ON THE FEEDBACK ON YOUR COURSEWORK

How to use markers' comments to develop your academic writing

Markers may provide comments on a standard feedback sheet or add handwritten notes on your script. Sometimes they may do both. It is essential that you learn from this feedback if you want to improve. This chapter outlines some common markers' annotations and describes how you should react to them.

KEY TOPICS

→ Types of feedback

→ Examples of feedback comments and what they mean

KEY UNIVERSITY TERMS

Annotation   Formative assessment   Summative assessment

Taking account of feedback from your tutors is a vitally important way of developing your writing skills. Their comments will help you appreciate the style and depth of thought expected in your work. At its simplest, feedback consists of the grade given to your assignments (or exam scripts, **Ch 19**) – you can often use this in conjunction with marking criteria (**Ch 14**) to find out where you might improve. In addition, markers' comments on your paper or script can provide more personalised feedback about your work. It is essential for your progress that you take a candid and even self-critical look at this sort of feedback to understand where you have scored highly or where your text was weak in content, structure or presentation.

Markers will have given your work their undivided attention and a lot of consideration to its strengths and weaknesses before awarding the grade. Their conclusions will come from long experience in their field as well as from reading many student assignments. Some students fail to collect their marked work and so deprive themselves of an excellent opportunity to gain insights about how their writing and, hence, how the content of their work might be improved for their next submission. The importance of considering and reacting to feedback is **Step 11** in the 12-step writing process (**Table 1.1**) and is addressed in this chapter.

TYPES OF FEEDBACK

The simplest pointer from any type of assessment is the grade you receive; if good, you know that you have reached the expected standard; if poor, you know that you should try to improve. If you feel unsure about the grading system or what standard is expected at each grading level, your course or school handbooks will probably include a description of marking or assessment criteria that explain this (**Ch 14**).

Written feedback may be provided directly on your essay, assignment or exam script. This will often take the form of handwritten comments over your text, and a summary commenting on your work or justifying why it received the mark it did. Sometimes the feedback will be provided separately from your work so that other markers are not influenced by others' comments.

Some feedback may be informal, for example, a tutor's personal notes on an assignment, or a comment about your contribution during a tutorial. If you feel uncertain about why your work has received the grade it did, or why a particular comment was provided, you may be able to arrange a one-to-one meeting with the person who marked your work. Normally they will be happy to provide further oral explanations. However, do not attempt to haggle over your marks, other than to point out politely if it seems that part of your work does not appear to have been marked at all, or part marks appear to have been added up wrongly.

EXAMPLES OF FEEDBACK COMMENTS AND WHAT THEY MEAN

Different lecturers use different terms to express similar meanings, and because they need to mark to a deadline, their handwritten comments are sometimes untidy and may be difficult to interpret.

Always read your feedback

Regardless of your grade, all comments in your feedback should give you constructive direction for later efforts and are designed to help you to develop the structure and style of your work, as well as encourage you to develop a deeper understanding of the topic. Where students ignore points, especially those about presentation or structure, then they may find themselves heavily penalised in later submissions.

Table 18.1 illustrates feedback comments that are frequently made and explains how you should react to obtain better grades in future. This should be viewed alongside **Table 17.3** which explains some proof-reading symbols that lecturers may use. If a particular comment or mark still does not make sense to you after reading these tables, then you may wish to approach the marker for an explanation.

Table 18.1 Common types of feedback annotation relating to content, structure and presentation, with suggested responses. Comments in the margin may be accompanied by underlining of word(s), circling of phrases, sentences or paragraphs.

Types of comment and typical examples	Meaning and potential remedial action
CONTENT	
Relevance *Relevance?* *Importance?* *Value of example?* *So?*	An example or quotation may not be apt, or you may not have explained its relevance. Think about the logic of your narrative or argument and whether there is a mismatch as implied, or whether you could add further explanation; choose a more appropriate example or quote.
Detail *Give more information* *Example?* *Too much detail/waffle/padding*	You are expected to flesh out your answer with more detail or an example to illustrate your point; or, conversely, you may have provided too much information. It may be that your work lacks substance and you appear to have compensated by putting in too much description rather than analysis, for example.
Specific factual comment or comment on your approach *You could have included ...* *What about ...?* *Why didn't you ...?*	Depends on context, but it should be obvious what is required to accommodate the comment.

Table 18.1 continued

Types of comment and typical examples	Meaning and potential remedial action
CONTENT (continued)	
Expressions of approval *Good!* *Excellent!* ✓ (may be repeated)	You got this right or chose a good example. Keep up the good work!
Expressions of disapproval *Poor* *Weak* *No!* ✗ (may be repeated)	Sometimes obvious, but may not be clear. The implication is that your examples, logic or use of specialist language could be improved. You need to think about this more deeply.
REGARDING STRUCTURE	
Fault in logic or argument *Logic!* *Non sequitur* (does not follow)	Your argument or line of logic is faulty. This may require quite radical changes to your approach to the topic.
Failure to introduce topic clearly *Where are you going with this?* *Unclear*	What is your understanding of the task? What parameters will confine your response? How do you intend to tackle the subject?
Failure to construct a logical discussion *Imbalanced discussion* *Weak on pros and cons*	When you have to compare and contrast in any way, then it is important that you give each element in your discussion equal coverage.
Failure to conclude essay clearly *So what?* *Conclusion?*	You have to leave a 'take-home message' that sums up the most salient features of your writing and you should not include new material in this section. This is to demonstrate your ability to think critically and define the key aspects.
Heavy dependency on quotations *Watch out for over-quotation* *Too many quotations*	There is a real danger of plagiarism if you include too many direct quotations from text. You have to demonstrate that you can synthesise the information from sources as evidence of your understanding. However, in a subject like English literature or law, quotation may be a key characteristic of writing. In this case, quotation is permitted, provided that it is supported by critical comment (**Ch 17** and **Ch 18**).
Move text *Loops and arrows*	Suggestion for changing order of text, usually to enhance the flow or logic.

Table 18.1 continued

Types of comment and typical examples	Meaning and potential remedial action
PRESENTATION	
Minor proofing errors sp. (usually in margin – spelling) 入 (insert material here) ⌐ (break paragraph here) ⁊ (delete this material) P (punctuation error)	A (minor) correction is required. Table 17.3 provides more detail of likely proof-reading symbols.
Citations Reference (required) Reference (or bibliography) list omitted Ref!	You have not supported evidence, argument or quotation with a reference to the original source. This is important in academic work and if you fail to do it, you may be considered guilty of plagiarism (Ch 17). If you omit a reference list, this will lose you marks as it implies a totally unsourced piece of writing, that is, you have done no specialist reading.
Tidiness Illegible! Untidy Can't read	Your handwriting may be difficult to decipher. Allocate more time to writing out your work neatly, or use a word processor if allowed. In exams you need to ensure that your hand-writing is legible otherwise you may lose marks.
Failure to follow recommended format Please follow departmental template for reports Order!	If the department or school provides a template for the submission of reports, then you must follow it. There are good reasons, such as the need to follow professional conventions, especially in sciences; you must conform. If you don't, then you may lose marks.

 PRACTICAL TIPS FOR ACTING ON FEEDBACK

Be mentally prepared to learn from the views of your tutors. You may initially feel that feedback is unfair, harsh or that it misunderstands the approach you were trying to take to the question. A natural reaction might be to dismiss many of the comments. However, you should recognise that tutors probably have a much deeper understanding of the topic than you, and concede that if you want to do well in a subject then you need to gain a better understanding of what makes a good answer from the academic's point of view.

Compare feedback with a study buddy or group of academic friends. It's always instructive to see comments on others' work. There may be praise for elements you didn't include or criticism for mistakes you missed. You may also learn from any stylistic, organisational or presentational differences they may have taken in their approaches to the assignment – and the marker's comments on these. As a pair or small group, you can increase the value of feedback by discussing why you took differing approaches and how well you feel they worked in the context of your tutor's comments and the marks received.

Look critically at your feedback. Separate out the comments on presentational/mechanical aspects from any points made about content, structure and logic. The first group can probably be easily remedied; the structural and content aspects may mean that you need to look at the balance between description, analysis and construction of your argument and the supporting evidence you have provided. If there is too much description, then you may have lost marks because that could have reduced the space you spent on the discussion that would have earned you more marks.

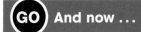 **And now ...**

18.1 Check out your department, school or faculty's marking criteria. As explained above, these may help you interpret feedback and understand how to reach the standard you want to achieve.

18.2 Decide what to do about feedback comments you frequently receive. Do lecturers always comment about your spelling or grammar; or suggest you should use more examples; or ask for more citations to be included? If so, look at relevant chapters and appendices in this book to see if you can adjust appropriately, or seek help from a tutor or academic support services.

18.3 Learn to criticise drafts of your own work. This is equivalent to giving feedback to yourself and is an essential academic skill. Annotate drafts of your own work – an important way to refine it and improve its quality. Stages for reviewing your written work are examined in **Ch 17**.

19

ACADEMIC WRITING IN EXAMS

How to translate the techniques of coursework writing into your exam script

The practice gained in constructing written coursework develops the skill of writing that helps you to write well under pressure within exam time limits. This chapter provides tips for writing answers quickly and effectively so that you can maximise the marks you obtain.

KEY TOPICS

➔ What lecturers are looking for in essay-style answers in exams

➔ Planning essay-style answers in exams

➔ The importance of addressing the question

➔ Providing evidence of deep thinking

➔ Reviewing your answers to gain marks

KEY UNIVERSITY TERMS

Instruction words   Personal pronoun   Rubric   Value judgement

In particular, this chapter addresses **Step 12**, the final step in the writing process (**Ch 1**), where you need to modify your writing technique to suit the mode required in exam answers. Writing under exam conditions imposes pressures – for instance, time limitations, memory and understanding, as well as your ability to formulate ideas and write about them quickly. Pre-exam practice is an obvious activity, but many students forget, or don't realise, that scrutinising feedback provided on coursework can give you insights on:

● things you have done well

● things you have done less well, especially with regard to content – and your interpretation of it compared to that of your tutor

● flaws in your understanding, explanation or use of evidence

- alternative views that might be obtained by further reading and
- weaknesses in your writing style and accuracy of language use, including spelling, punctuation and word choices.

Revisiting the feedback on all your assignments will give you general pointers that might apply to all your exams.

WHAT LECTURERS ARE LOOKING FOR IN ESSAY-STYLE ANSWERS IN EXAMS

Essay-style questions are mainly used by tutors to elicit an in-depth answer to a complex issue. Other shorter forms, such as multiple–choice or short-answer questions, tend to be included when they want you to address knowledge over a wide area, whereas the essay format allows you to develop an argument, explain alternative views or provide a high level of detail to demonstrate understanding in your answer. Since you cannot be expected to know all topics in this sort of depth, there is often an element of choice in essay exam papers.

 Critical thinking

Essays are commonly used when tutors expect you to think more deeply. Often what you have to do is not framed as a question but an instruction. Typically, you will be expected to:

- **apply** knowledge and understanding
- **analyse** information
- **synthesise** new ideas or treatments of facts
- **evaluate** issues, positions and arguments.

Table 11.2 gives further explanation of what's expected under these headings, and watch out for instruction words that invite these approaches.

PLANNING ESSAY-STYLE ANSWERS IN EXAMS

The key tip is to keep your writing simple. Working quickly, use a concept diagram (or mind map) to generate ideas relevant to the question. From this, decide on an outline structure. This approach helps you to think laterally as well as in a linear manner – important so that you generate all the points relevant to your answer. As explained in **Chapter 9**, you should probably think in terms of three basic components.

- **The introduction:** states briefly what your answer will say, sets its context and indicates how you intend to approach the topic.

- **The main body:** presents the information, the argument or key points of your response.

- **The conclusion:** sums up the answer as stated, reinforces the position outlined in the introduction, and puts the whole answer into a wider context.

Tips for writing these elements are provided in **Chapter 9**, while potential ways of organising the main body of essay-style assignments are discussed in **Chapter 15**.

Table 19.1 describes some common faults that can occur when students fail to consider the structure of their writing. An important way in which marks can be lost is through poor structuring of exam answers. Ideally, your outline plan will lead to an obvious structure for the main body of the text, but often in exam situations, a piece of writing evolves once the writer begins to write. This is because the act of writing stimulates development of thought, potentially leading to changes in order and in content. In these cases, your initial outline plan should be seen as a flexible guideline that may change as you begin to think more deeply about the topic.

On the other hand, if the planning phase is ignored completely, and you only think about the structure while you write, then you can end up with a weakly structured essay. It is perfectly acceptable practice to make notes in exam books; however, you should always score through them before you submit the answer paper. A single diagonal line will suffice. Sometimes your plan may be used by the examiner to cross-check details of your answer (but do not count on this).

Table 19.1 Common faults in the structure of essay-style answers in exams. In most of these examples, paying more attention to the planning phase in the exam will result in a better structure, and, hence, better marks.

Symptom of weakness in structure	Analysis of the problem
The magical mystery tour. This type of answer rambles on, drifting from point to disconnected point with no real structure.	The essay may contain valuable content, but marks will be lost because this is not organised and parts are not connected appropriately to create a coherent response.
No introduction and/or no conclusion. The main body contains many useful points, but fails to introduce them and fails to draw conclusions based on them.	Facts, concepts and ideas alone are not enough – evidence must be provided of deeper-level analytical thinking (Ch 11). The introduction and conclusions are important areas where this can be achieved.
The overly-detailed answer. The main body of the answer contains a wealth of information, some of which is relevant and some not. Despite the finely-grained detail, little structure is evident and there is no discrimination between the important and the unimportant.	The writer has probably been preoccupied with showing how much has been memorised, without showing how much has been understood. Relevance of the material in relation to the instruction given has not been considered at the planning stage, or as the essay-writing progresses.
The stream of consciousness. Often written as if it were a conversational monologue, this lacks internal organisation, few (or too many) signposting words, no (or few) paragraphs, and little apparent logic.	Academic writing style involves structural as well as linguistic components. Both are important elements of a good answer. Hence, the writing needs to guide the reader along a logical path to enable understanding.
The waffly, irrelevant answer. Unfocussed, fails to get to grips with the question and may contain large amounts of irrelevant information, offered up seemingly without regard for the topic set.	Greater attention needs to be paid to analysis of the instruction given and converting these thoughts into a coherent answer plan. Irrelevant material should not be used as it will gain no marks.
The half-an-answer. Fails to appreciate that there were two (or more) parts to the question. Focusses solely on the first part.	The answer should cover all aspects of the question as more marks may be allocated to the secondary part(s). This should be reflected in your plan and the eventual structure.
Text dominated by quotes. This might start with a hackneyed quote or be interspersed with extensive memorised quotes or references, with little effective use of these.	This type of structure leaves little room for evidence of original thought. Few marks are given for having a good memory – it's what is done with the information that counts.

THE IMPORTANCE OF ADDRESSING THE QUESTION

Another important way in which marks can be lost is when answers do not address the task as set (see Table 19.2). You can avoid this by:

- making sure you consider all aspects of the question. Brainstorming techniques (**Ch 15** and **Figure A2.5**) can help you achieve this

- explaining what *you* understand by the question (perhaps in the introductory paragraph). This will make you think about the question and may clear up any doubt about how it can be interpreted. However, make sure you do not narrow the topic beyond what would be reasonable

- focussing on the precise task you have been asked to do (**Ch 8**). Remember to tackle the question actually asked and not the one you would have liked to answer – this is a risk of question-spotting

- ensuring your answer is planned. Creating a plan will make you think about relevance and the logic of your argument (**Chs 9**, **10** and **15**)

- keeping to the point. Including irrelevant or repetitive content will not gain any marks and the time you spend writing it will be wasted, stopping you from gaining marks on other questions. Having said that, no marks are given for 'white space'; even a few general points of principle may result in enough marks to help you pass, when added to those gained in other, better, answers

- making sure you answer all parts in multi-part questions. These may not be worded in two or more sentences: phrases such as 'compare and contrast' and 'cause and effect' should alert you to this. Make sure that the weighting in marks given to questions is reflected in the length of the component parts of your answer so that you do not address one part exhaustively and fail to cover the remaining part(s) entirely or only superficially

- avoiding making unsupported value judgements. These are statements that impose the writer's views on the reader, often using subjective language, and which fail to provide sound evidence to support the position put forward (**Ch 11**)

- writing objectively and avoiding using the personal pronouns 'I', 'you', 'we' and 'one' (unless you have been asked specifically to take a reflective view of your role in a situation).

Table 19.2 Checklist of possible reasons for poor exam marks in exam essays. Use this list to identify where you may have been at fault.

Reason
Not answering the exact question as set: • failing to carry out the precise instruction in a question • failing to recognise the specialist terms used in the question • failing to address all aspects of the question
Poor time management: • failing to match the extent of the answer(s) to the time allocated • spending too long on one question and not enough on the others
Failing to weight parts of the answer appropriately: not recognising that one aspect (perhaps involving more complex ideas) may carry more marks than another
Failing to provide evidence to support an answer: not including examples or stating the 'obvious' – like basic facts or definitions
Failing to illustrate an answer appropriately: • not including a relevant diagram • providing a diagram that does not aid communication
Incomplete or shallow answers: • failing to answer appropriately due to lack of knowledge • not considering the topic in sufficient depth
Providing irrelevant evidence to support an answer: 'waffling' to fill space
Illegible handwriting: if it can't be read, it can't be marked
Poor English: facts and ideas are not expressed clearly; poor use of language
Lack of logic or structure to the answer: a plan not used or structure not evident
Factual errors: problems with note-taking, learning, revision or recall
Failing to correct obvious mistakes: lack of time allocated to proof-reading your answer

 Quotations and citations in exam answers

Do not become bogged down in trying to remember direct quotes word for word (possible exceptions are in literature and law exams). Just give the sense of the quote, its relevance to your answer and its source.

Analysing the wording of each question

Chapter 8 explained how analysis of the question wording requires a bit more than simply thinking about *what* you are being asked to do. You need to take a broader and more in-depth look at the task in the context of the whole question. To do this, you must consider:

■ **The instruction word.** In what category does that place the task? For example, have you been asked to act, describe, analyse, argue, or do something else completely (**Ch 8**)?

■ **The topic.** What is the core topic about?

■ **The aspect(s) to be covered.** What particular aspect of the topic has to be considered?

■ **Any restriction(s).** What limits have been imposed on the discussion? Your answer must encompass each element of the task to ensure that it is a logical, relevant response to the task you were set. Superfluous material or digressions will not earn you marks.

PROVIDING EVIDENCE OF DEEP THINKING

Especially at higher levels of study, you will need to provide evidence of deep thinking to gain good grades. On the assumption that you are able to include basic information and display an understanding of it, you can gain marks for:

● supplying additional and relevant detail at the expected depth

● providing an analytical answer rather than a descriptive one – covering deeper aspects, rather than merely recounting facts

● setting a problem in context, and demonstrating a wider understanding of the topic. However, make sure you don't overdo this, or you may risk not answering the question as set – remember that you cannot be expected to give the same amount of detail in an exam answer as you would in a piece of essay-style coursework

● giving evidence of reading around the subject – quote relevant papers and reviews, mention author names and dates of publication

● considering all sides of a topic/debate, and arriving at a clear conclusion – you may have to take into account and explain two or more viewpoints, and possibly weigh them up, according to the question as set. Where appropriate, your answer should demonstrate that you realise that the issue is complex and possibly unresolved.

Try to to help staff to help you

It's important to realise that the person who marks your work is not an adversary. Most lecturers are disappointed when giving students a poor grade, but they approach the marking process professionally and with ruthless objectivity. Tutors are often very frustrated when they see that simple changes in approach might have led to a better mark, and they cannot assume that you know things that you do not put down on paper.

REVIEWING YOUR ANSWERS TO GAIN MARKS

This is an essential stage of creating a sound piece of academic writing, whether for an in-course assignment or exam (**Ch 19**). Many students want to get out of the exam room as soon as possible, but you should not do this unless you are convinced you have squeezed every last mark out of the paper. Your exam strategy should always include an allocation of time for reviewing. Trapping simple errors could mean the difference between a pass or a fail or between degree classifications. These are some of the things you could look for when reviewing your work (**Ch 17**):

- Basics. Make sure you have numbered your answers, answered the right number of questions, and have followed the instructions in the rubric at the start of the paper.

- Spelling, grammar and sense. Quickly read through your answer critically (try to imagine it has been written by someone else) and correct any obvious errors that strike you. Does the text make sense? Do the sentences and paragraphs flow smoothly?

- Structure and relevance. Once again, ask yourself whether you have really answered the question that was set. Have you followed precisely the instruction(s) in the title? Is anything missed out? Are the different parts linked together well? Look for inconsistencies in argument. Add new material if necessary.

'Small-scale' corrections like spelling errors and changes to punctuation marks can be made directly in your text using standard proof-reading symbols if required (**Ch 17**).

Strategies to help you before the exam

■ Create your revision timetable with time available to allow for practice, then with a friend, test yourself on the straight recall of basic facts

■ Analyse past papers to identify the style of paper, types of questions and the time that you could allocate to each in the exam, remembering to allow time for planning and checking your answers

■ Create practice plans for different questions or tasks from some of the recent past papers. As you become better at this, you'll be able to create a plan in the same time that you could allocate to this in the exam. Test yourself against the clock

■ Practise writing up a full answer against the clock. This will show you how much you can write in longhand in the time available

■ Use your practice plans and answers as revision aids. You'll be able to modify your plan to meet the needs of similar questions in your exam and you won't have to think up your answer from scratch.

Strategies to help your marker in the exam

Working under pressure can mean that handwriting becomes less well formed and so you need to make sure that words are legible. If you have used non-standard 'shorthand' expressions e.g. 'govt' for 'government', then make it clear in the text what the abbreviation means. Be sure to annotate your script clearly. As you skim-read your answers you can make adjustments. Sometimes, this will simply mean inserting a mark (ʎ or ^) between words and writing a missing word or phrase in the space above. In other instances, you can insert ʎ or ^ and write 'see additional paragraph x at *** (which you can add either on the facing page or at the end of that particular answer).

 PRACTICAL TIPS FOR BOOSTING YOUR EXAM MARKS

Go in well prepared. Of course, you'd expect any lecturer to say this, because in terms of gaining good marks, there is no substitute for effective revision. However, being well prepared means more than memorising facts and concepts. To do well you also need to arrive at the exam room in a good mental state, with a plan and a positive attitude and the determination to get down to work quickly and effectively.

Convert your brainstorm into a plan as quickly as possible. You can do this very quickly simply by numbering the headings in the brainstorm in the order you intend to write about them (**Figure A2.5**).

Balance your effort appropriately. For example, in exam answers your introduction need not be overly long. Most marks will be awarded for the main body and conclusions, so spend more time and brainpower on them.

Factor in time to allow you to review your script. When working out how long you can afford to spend on each element of your exam paper, include some time for checking it over. It is probably better to keep this as a chunk of time towards the end of the exam as this will mean that you will have completed the paper in its entirety and it will have given you a break between writing the response and carrying out your review/edit/proof stages.

Keep your writing simple. If you are to stick to your exam strategy, you must not lose valuable time creating an attention-grabbing piece of writing. You won't have time or space to refine your answer in the same way as you would with a piece of coursework. In particular, don't labour the introduction with fine phrases – get straight to the point of the question and give your response to it.

Look out for repeated errors. Under pressure, students sometimes find that they have consistently made an error, for example, referred to Louis XIV throughout as Louis XVI or written 'Louise' rather than 'Louis'. If this happens to you, then just put an asterisk (*) beside the first occurrence of the error and add a note at the end of your answer or in the margin for example: *consistent error. Please read as 'Louis XIV' throughout*. Note that you will not lose marks for correcting your work in this way.

(GO) And now ...

19.1 Review essay-style questions in past exam papers. Look at these particularly from the point of view of the depth of answers required. Consider both the instruction word used (**Table 8.2**) and the context to gain an appreciation of the level of thinking demanded. Consult **Table 11.2** if you need to review 'thinking processes'.

19.2 Focus on definitions and possible formats during revision. If you have trouble getting your answers started during exams, it can be a useful device to start with a definition; alternatively, think about stating the situation, the problem and then the potential solution (Table 15.1). This might not be applicable to all scenarios, but if you are really stuck this will at least give you a framework for thinking and writing.

19.3 Use formative assessment exercises to improve your English. If you recognise that your use of language is weak, then take advantage of all formative assessment exercises to help you improve. Speak with markers and tutors about how you might enhance your marks. If your use of language is seen as an impediment to your performance, seek advice from your student advisory service. Many universities have academic writing advisors who can help with specific writing problems.

Further detailed information about the issues in this chapter can be found in McMillan and Weyers, 2010. How to succeed in exams and assessments.

APPENDICES

APPENDIX 1
SPEED-READING TECHNIQUES

Speed-reading is a useful skill for students as they need to decide quickly on the relevance of a text to their academic work. To learn how to improve reading speed, it helps to understand how fast readers 'operate'. Instead of reading each word as a separate unit, these readers use peripheral vision (what is seen, while staring ahead, at the furthest extreme to the right and the left). They absorb clusters of words in one 'flash' or 'fixation' on the text (**Figure A1.1a**). In this example, four fixations are required to read that single line of text. A reader who does this is reading more efficiently than the reader who reads word-by-word (**Figure A1.1b**). This reader makes 12 fixations along the line, which means that their reading efficiency is low. Research indicates that people who read slowly in this way are less likely to absorb information quickly enough for the brain to comprehend. Thus reading slowly can actually hinder rather than aid understanding.

As a practised reader, you will probably have developed these fast-reading skills to some degree. They can be improved using techniques like the 'eye gymnastic' exercise in **Figure A1.2**. Other things you can do include 'finger tracing', where you run your finger below the line of text being read to follow your eye's path across a page, starting and stopping a word or two from either side. This is said to increase your eye speed, keep your mind focussed on the words being read and prevent you from skipping back to previous sentences or jumping forward to text that follows.

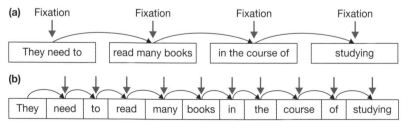

Figure A1.1 Eye movements when reading. (a) reader who makes eye fixations on clusters of words. (b) reader who reads every word one-by-one.

Learning to read quickly	is a skill	that needs to be developed.
If you have to read	a new piece of text,	you will find it useful
first of all	to read	the first paragraph
and the last paragraph	of the section, chapter or article.	From this
you should be able	to gauge	the context
and general outline	of the topic under discussion.	While it is true
that all academic texts	should have been well edited	before publication,
it does not follow	that every text	will follow these conventions.
However,	a well-written piece	of academic writing
should follow this pattern	and, as a reader,	you should exploit
this convention	in order to help you	to understand
the overall content	before you embark	on intensive reading
of the text.		

When you are about to	make notes from texts	you should not begin
by sitting	with notepad ready	and the pen poised.
Certainly	make a note of	publication details needed
for your bibliography,	but resist the temptation	to start taking notes
at the same time as	beginning	your first reading of the text.
It is better	to read first,	reflect, recall
and then write notes	based on	what you remember.
This gives you	a framework	around which
you ought to be able	to organise your notes	after you have read
the text intensively.	People who start	by writing notes
as soon as	they open the book	will end up
copying	more and more from the text	as their tiredness increases.
In this case	very little	reflection or learning
is achieved.		

Figure A1.2 'Eye gymnastics' exercise. Try to read the following text quite quickly. Read from left to right in the normal way. The aim of the activity is to train your eyes to make more use of your peripheral vision when you are reading. In this way, you will learn to make fewer fixations on the text by forcing your eyes to focus on the centre of a group of words, which are printed in naturally occurring clusters – usually on the basis of grammatical or logical framing. It may be that you experience some discomfort behind your eyes, which indicates that they are adjusting to this less familiar pattern. If this is the case, you should keep practising using this text as a means of developing the speed of your eye movements.

Some people find it helpful to use a bookmark placed horizontally along the line they are reading as a useful guide that prevents the eye jumping ahead of the text they are reading.

The average reading speed is said to be 265 words per minute (wpm). Reading speed for university students may be slightly lower, as aspects like difficulty of the text, unfamiliarity with the terminology used and the complexity of the concepts being discussed in the text have the potential to slow down reading. As you become more familiar with the subject and the issues being covered in your course and, thus, with your supplementary reading, then your reading speed will increase.

You can assess your normal reading speed using either method described in **Table A1.1**. If your reading speed seems slow, then you can work on improving this by using a similar level and length text at the same time each day. Go through the reading speed process and, gradually, you should see your average reading speed improve.

Table A1.1 **How to calculate your reading speed.** These two examples show how to do this calculation.

Method A (specified reading time)	
a Select a chapter from a textbook. (This is better than a newspaper or journal because these are often printed in columns.)	
b Calculate the average number of words per line e.g. 50 words counted over 5 lines	= 10 words per line
c Count number of lines per page	= 41 total lines
d Multiply (b x c) = 10 $\times$ 45	= 410 words per page
e Read for specific time (to nearest minute or half-minute) without stopping	= 4 minutes reading
f Number of pages read in 4 minutes	= 2½ (2.5) pages read
g Multiply (d $\times$ f) = 410 x 2.5	= 1025 total words read
h Divide (g by e) = 1025 $\times$ 4	= **256 words per minute**
Method B (specified text length)	
a Find piece of text of known or estimated word length (see Method A)	= 744 words
b Note time taken to read this in seconds	= 170 seconds
c Convert seconds to decimal fraction of minutes = 170 $\div$ 60	= 2.8 minutes
d Divide (a by c) = 744 $\times$ 2.8	= **266 words per minute**

Increasing your reading speed using finger tracing

Try the following method.

■ Select a reading passage of about two pages in length. Note your starting and finishing times and calculate your reading speed using Method B in **Table A1.1**.

■ Take a break of 40–60 minutes.

■ Return to the text and run a finger along the line of text much faster than you could possibly read it.

■ Repeat, but more slowly, so that you can just read it ('finger tracing'). Again, note your starting and finishing times, and work out your reading speed. You should find that your reading speed has increased from the first reading.

■ Carry out this exercise at the same time of day over a week using texts of similar length and complexity to help you increase your reading speed.

There are many other strategies you can develop to read and absorb content quickly. These include:

● **Skimming** – pick out a specific piece of information by quickly letting the eye run down a list or over a page looking for a key word or phrase, as when seeking a particular word in an index.

● **Scanning** – let your eye run quickly over a chapter, for example, before you commit yourself to study-read the whole text. This will help you to gain an overview of the chapter before you start.

● **Picking out the topic sentences** – as seen in **Figure 5.1** and **Example 5.1**, by reading the topic sentences you will be able to flesh out your overview of the text content. This will aid your understanding before you study-read the whole text.

● **Identifying the signpost words** – as noted in **Chapter 5** and in **Table 16.2**, these help guide you as the reader through the logical process that the author has mapped out for you.

● **Recognising clusters of grammatically allied words** – subliminally, you will be grouping words in clusters according to their natural alliances. This will help you to read by making fewer fixations and this will improve your reading speed. You can improve your speed at doing this by using the eye-gymnastic exercise described later.

Things that can reduce your reading speed

As well as trying methods to read faster, you should be aware of circumstances that might slow you down. These include:

- distractions such as background noise of television, music or chatter
- sub-vocalisation (sounding out each word as it is read aloud)
- reading word-by-word
- over-tiredness
- poor eye-sight – if you think your eyes are not 20:20, then it might be worth going for an eye test. your eyes are too important to neglect and a pair of reading glasses may make a huge difference to your studying comfort
- poor lighting – if you can, read using a lamp that can shine directly on the text. reading in poor light causes eye-strain, and this can limit concentration and the length of reading episodes.

● **Taking cues from punctuation** – as you read, you will gain some understanding by interpreting the text using the cues of full-stops and commas, for example, to help you gain understanding of what you are reading. The importance of punctuation to comprehension is vital (**Appendix 2**).

To be effective, reading quickly must be matched by a good level of comprehension. Conversely, as noted already reading too slowly can mean that comprehension is hampered. Clearly, you need to incorporate tests of your understanding to check that you have understood the main points of the text. You might do this by reading a section, leaving the task for a short time, then making notes of key points you recollect from the text. Check your notes against the content. If you have been unsuccessful in remembering key points or have only partial recollection, then re-read the text and repeat the process. In this way you will begin to read more actively. This is also a helpful strategy when revising for exams.

APPENDIX 2
EXAMPLES OF NOTE-CREATION STYLES

Note-creation needs to be suited to the learning style of the student, the context (from reading or from lectures, for example), the subject matter, the purpose in recording the information and the time available for note creation. **Table A2.1** compares seven different approaches and presents some of their advantages and disadvantages. These are modelled later in this Appendix and, at particular times, some styles may be more suited to your purpose or situation than others.

Table A2.1 A comparison of the different methods of creating notes as illustrated in Figures A2.1–A2.7 below

Note type	Figure	Advantage	Disadvantage
Keyword notes	A2.1	Good as a layout for easy access to information	Dependent on systematic structure in text
Linear notes	A2.2	Numbered sequence – good for classifying ideas	Restrictive format, difficult to backtrack to insert new information
Time lines	A2.3	Act as memory aid for a sequence of events; stages in a process	Limited information possible
Flow-chart notes	A2.4	Allow clear path through complex options	Take up space; may be unwieldy
Concept maps/ mind maps	A2.5	Good for recording information on a single page	Can become messy; can be difficult to follow; not suited to all learning styles
Matrix notes/grid notes	A2.6	Good layout for recording different viewpoints, approaches, applications	Space limitations on content or amount of information
Herringbone maps	A2.7	Good for laying out opposing sides of an argument	Space limitations on content or amount of information

Topic: DEPOPULATION OF THE COUNTRYSIDE		Source: Ormiston, J., 2002. Rural Idylls. Glasgow: Country Press.
Problem:	Population falling in rural areas Traditional communities disintegrate Incomer settlement – dormitory villages	
Reasons:	Mechanisation of farming Creation of farming combines Bigger farms, fewer employed Decline of traditional farming & related activities	
Effects:	Families dispersed – fewer children Closure of shops, post offices, schools, surgeries Transport links less viable	
Solutions:	Housing subsidies to encourage families to remain Diversify economic activity, e.g. tourism/action holidays Stimulate rural economy – farm shops, farmers' markets Diversify from traditional crops – seek new markets	

Figure A2.1 Example of keyword notes.

Topic: OBESITY IN CHILDREN — *Source: Skinner, J., 2001. Diet and Obesity. Edinburgh: Castle Publishing.*

1. Lifestyle
   - 1.1 Television, computer-games generation
   - 1.2 Unsupervised leisure time – sedentary
2. Diet
   - 2.1 Constant 'grazing' – junk food
   - 2.2 Additives/processed foods
   - 2.3 Lack of adequate fresh food, including fruit + vegetables
3. Exercise
   - 3.1 Sport by spectating rather than participating
   - 3.2 Decline in team sports in schools
   - 3.3 Children over-protected from 'free play' outdoors
4. Family
   - 4.1 Parents overeat; children likewise
   - 4.2 Instant food
   - 4.3 Food as an incentive + reward
5. Schools
   - 5.1 School meals spurned in favour of snack bar/chip shop
   - 5.2 Healthy-eating programmes as part of curriculum
6. Health service
   - 6.1 Less emphasis on prevention
   - 6.2 Limited health education of parents and children

(a)

Figure A2.2 Examples of linear notes. These are samples drawn from three diverse disciplines (a, b, and c) where topics lend themselves to hierarchical approaches.

Figure A2.2 continued

Topic:

GENERAL FEATURES OF ORGANIC MATERIALS

Source: Barker, J., 2001. Chemistry for University. Manchester: Midland Publishing.

1. Solid state – molec. crystal – powder, poly. Thin films
2. Unique physical properties – exploit for high-tech applications
3. Advantages
   - 3.1 Versatile properties – reg. by organic chemistry
   - 3.2 Readily accessible – via organic synthesis
   - 3.3 Low cost – cheap raw materials
   - 3.4 Tractable – fusable, soluble: easy to fab.
4. Disadvantage
   - 4.1 Relatively fragile
5. Important types
   - 5.1 Conducting CT salts
   - 5.2 Conducting poly

(b)

Topic: **OPERATIONAL AMPLIFIERS**

Source: Scott, D.I., 1977. Operational Amplifiers. Coventry: Circuit Publishers.

1. Usually an integrated circuit; can be discrete
2. Uses all technologies: bipolar; FET; MOS; BI-FET
3. Effectively a highly stable differential amplifier
4. Advantages
   - 4.1 High voltage gain – typ. 100,000
   - 4.2 High input impedance – typ. 1MΩ – can be much higher, FET, MOS
   - 4.3 Low output impedance – typ. 600Ω
   - 4.4 Low drift, BI-FET best
   - 4.5 Wide supply voltage range
5. Disadvantages
   - 5.1 Relatively narrow bandwidth – GBP typ. 1MHz (but operates to DC)
   - 5.2 Very unstable in discrete versions – requires matched transistors
6. Common types
   - 6.1 741 – most common
   - 6.2 LM 380 – common AF AMP
   - 6.3 TDA 2030 – common power amp. – 20W into 4Ω

(c)

Figure A2.3 **Example of time-line notes.** This design is good for showing a sequence of events, in this case, the development of European organisations.

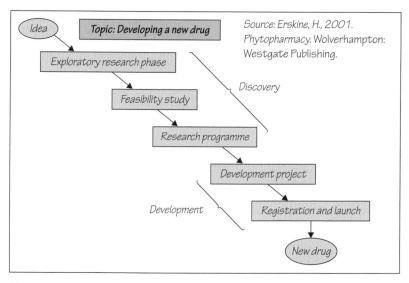

Figure A2.4 **Example of flow-chart notes.** These are particularly useful for describing complex processes in visual form.

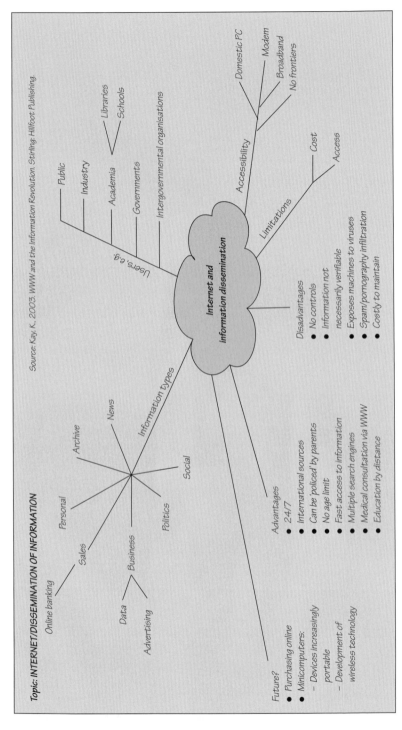

Topic: INTERNET/DISSEMINATION OF INFORMATION

Source: Kay, K. 2003. WWW and the Information Revolution. Stirling: Hillfoot Publishing.

Online banking

Personal

Sales

Data — Business

Advertising

Archive

News

Social

Politics

Information types

Users, e.g.:

Public

Industry

Academia — Libraries, Schools

Governments

Intergovernmental organisations

Accessibility — Domestic PC, Modem, Broadband, No frontiers

Limitations — Cost, Access

Internet and information dissemination

Advantages
• 24/7
• International sources
• Can be 'policed' by parents
• No age limit
• Fast access to information
• Multiple search engines
• Medical consultation via WWW
• Education by distance

Disadvantages
• No controls
• Information not necessarily verifiable
• Exposes machines to viruses
• Spam/pornography infiltration
• Costly to maintain

Future?
• Purchasing online
• Minicomputers:
– Devices increasingly portable
– Development of wireless technology

Figure A2.5 Example of a concept map. This may also be called a mind map. Suits visual-spatial/visual learners.

Topic: TRAFFIC CONGESTION

Source: Walker, I.M.A., 2005. Urban Myths and Motorists. London: Green Press.

Solutions	Council view	Police view	Local business view	Local community view
Pedestrianisation	+ Low maintenance − Initial outlay	+ Easier to police + Less car crime + CCTV surveillance easier	+ Safer shopping and business activity − Discourages motorist customers	+ Safer shopping + Less polluted town/city environment
Park and ride schemes	+ Implements transport policy − Capital investment to initiate − Car park maintenance	+ Reduce inner-city/town traffic jams + Reduce motor accidents − Potential car park crime	− Loss of custom − Lack of convenience − Sends customers elsewhere	+ Less polluted town/city environment − Costly
Increase parking charges	+ Revenue from fines − Costly to set up	− Hostility to enforcers	− Loss of custom − Delivery unloading problematic	− Residents penalised by paying for on-street parking
Restrict car journeys, e.g. odd/even registrations on alternate days	+ Easy to administer	+ Easy to police	− Seek exemption for business vehicles	+ Encourage car-sharing for daily journeys − Inconvenience
Levy congestion charge for urban journeys	+ Revenue raised − Cost of implementing tracking system	− Traffic jams on alternative routes	− Cost of loss of custom	− Inhibit work/leisure activities − Cost

Figure A2.6 Example of matrix notes. This particular analysis lays out positive (+) and negative (−) viewpoints on an issue from a range of different perspectives.

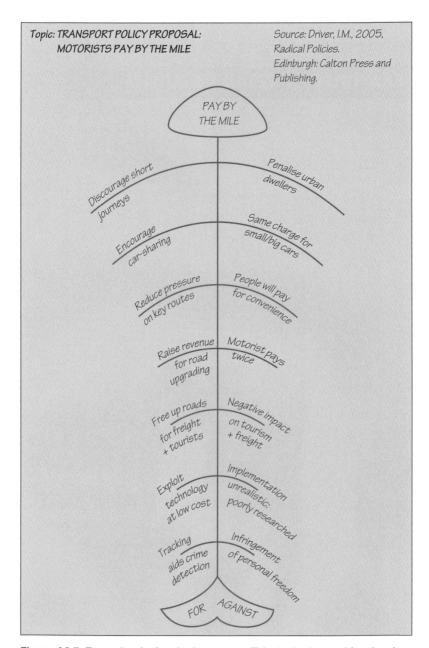

Topic: *TRANSPORT POLICY PROPOSAL:*
      MOTORISTS PAY BY THE MILE

Source: *Driver, I.M., 2005,*
Radical Policies.
Edinburgh: Calton Press and
Publishing.

PAY BY
THE MILE

Discourage short journeys

Penalise urban dwellers

Encourage car-sharing

Same charge for small/big cars

Reduce pressure on key routes

People will pay for convenience

Raise revenue for road upgrading

Motorist pays twice

Free up roads for freight + tourists

Negative impact on tourism + freight

Exploit technology at low cost

Implementation unrealistic: poorly researched

Tracking aids crime detection

Infringement of personal freedom

FOR   AGAINST

Figure A2.7 Example of a herringbone map. This design is good for showing, as in this case, two sides to an argument. It may be particularly appealing to visual learners.

APPENDIX 3 FALLACIES AND LOGIC: EXAMPLES OF WEAK THINKING

As you consider arguments and discussions on academic subjects, you will notice that various linguistic strategies are used to promote particular points of view. Recognising these is a valuable aspect of critical thinking needed for academic writing. The list below gives some of the more common examples of weak thinking.

- **Attacking an individual orally or in print.** The character of the person putting forward the argument is attacked, rather than the point that is being presented.

  e.g. *The President's moral behaviour is suspect, so his financial policies must also be dubious.*

  An appropriate reaction: suggest that the person's character or circumstances are irrelevant

- **Basing argument on a popular viewpoint.** Popularity of a viewpoint does not make it correct in itself.

  e.g. *The majority of people support corporal punishment for vandals, so we should introduce boot camps.*

  An appropriate reaction: watch out for bias, bandwagon and peer-pressure effects and ignore them when considering rights and wrongs.

- **I know someone who …** Using unrepresentative exceptions to contradict an argument based on statistical evidence.

  e.g. *My gran was a heavy smoker and she lived to be 95, so smoking won't harm me.*

  An appropriate reaction: consider the overall weight of evidence rather than isolated examples.

- **An important person said …** An argument is supported on the basis that an expert or authority agrees with the conclusion. A strategy often used in advertisements, where celebrity endorsement and testimonials are frequent.

  e.g. *My professor, whom I admire greatly, believes in Smith's theory, so it must be right.*

  An appropriate reaction: point out that experts do disagree and explain how and why; focus on the key qualities of the item or argument.

- **Citing negative evidence.** Since there is no evidence for (or against) a case, it means that the case must be false (or true).

  e.g. You haven't an alibi, therefore, you must be guilty.

  An appropriate reaction: point out that a conclusion either way may not be possible in the absence of evidence.

- **Biased evidence.** One-sided selection of examples for (or against a case) rely on bias to build an argument, for example, when a writer quotes one view, but not alternative views.

  e.g. My advisors tell me that global warming is not going to happen.

  An appropriate reaction: read around the subject, including sources offering different views and try to arrive at a balanced opinion.

- **Confusing or masking points by use of complex language.** Use of phrasing to hide the true position or exaggerate an opposing view, for example, stating things in mild, emotive or obscure language or using technical 'jargon' words to sound authoritative.

  e.g. My job as a vertical transportation operative means that I am used to being in a responsible position. (Am I a forklift truck operator or an airline pilot?)

  An appropriate reaction: watch for (unnecessary) adjectives, noun strings (as in the example above) or adverbs that may affect the way that you consider the evidence.

- **Repetition.** Saying the same thing over and over again, thus conditioning people to believe it. Common in politics, war propaganda and advertising.

  e.g. 'Beanz meanz Heinz.'

  An appropriate reaction: look out for repeated catchphrases and lack of substantive argument.

- **Diversionary arguments.** A position is misrepresented in order to create a diversionary debating point that is easily accepted or rejected, when, in fact, the core issue has not been addressed.

  e.g. Asylum seekers all want to milk the benefits system, so we should turn them all away.

  An appropriate reaction: point out the fallacy and focus on the core issue.

APPENDIX 4 SAMPLE PLAN FOR A STUDENT WRITING TASK

The plan below outlines a potential answer to the sample task in Appendix 4. Your plans might be less elaborate. The detail here is given to illustrate the method and logic that can be applied to planning and writing long texts. This topic could apply to a number of disciplines, for example, Accounting, Civil Engineering, Community Medicine, Design, Economics, Environmental Science, Geography, Law, Politics, Town Planning.

Sample task: Consider the implications of extreme flooding in the UK over the last decade.

MODEL RESPONSE

1. **INTRODUCTION** [General context ⇒ more specific ⇒ specific ⇒ intention]

1.1 Extreme flooding – phenomenon of last decade.

- When? 2007 and 2012–13
- Areas affected in UK: North-East Scotland, Scottish Borders, Yorkshire, Midlands, Wales, West country, Norfolk.

1.2 Causal factors

- freak weather conditions (could be attributable to global warming claims)
- higher than average rainfall over prolonged period
- cyclical weather patterns?

1.3 Consequences

- on reservoirs
- on inland rivers
- on flood plains
- on coastal areas

1.4 Implications for [main thrust of text – statement of intent]

1.4.1 **Environment**

- flora, fauna, river courses, aquifers etc.

1.4.2 Community

- local community
- business community
- farming community

1.4.2 Crisis management

- support services

1.4.3 Cost

- who pays?
- Government and local authorities
- insurance industry
- assessing compensation

1.4.4 Prevention

- changes in policies and action on protection the UK as a whole

MAIN BODY OF DISCUSSION [Items as outlined in 1.4 above]

2 ENVIRONMENT – impact

- damage to aquifers, ground surface, plant and wild life
- damage to communication infrastructure – rivers, canals, roads, bridges, railways
- damage to utilities infrastructure – fresh water, drainage, sewage, electrical power, telephone

Mini-conclusion: long-term impact with continuing threat of repetition

3. COMMUNITY

3.1 Local community

Residents – impact

- fabric of homes damaged
- loss of furnishings and irreplaceable personal possessions
- re-housing need – temporary but possibly long-term accommodation
- long-term loss of value of homes
- threat of repetition of flooding
- increase in insurance premiums

3.2 Business community

- loss of trade, thus, viability threatened
- reconstruction long-term thus ability to trade/function restricted
- impediments to transport of goods and services

3.3 Farming community

- damage to fishing/arable/livestock/crofting/tourism
- soil damaged by flooding
- fodder unusable – either buy in fodder or slaughter animals
- animals drowned or stranded
- financial loss

Mini-conclusion: financial implications, damage to local economy and livelihoods

4. CRISIS MANAGEMENT

4.1 Support services – roles of

- Department for Environment, Food and Rural Affairs for England and Wales (DEFRA)
- Scottish Environmental Protection Agency (SEPA)
- Emergency Services – Police, Fire, Ambulance, Coastguard, Lifeboat, Search and Rescue
- Utilities e.g. water, sewage, electrical power, gas
- set up initiatives to replace/supplement damaged industries/ economic activity

Mini-conclusion: need for specialist equipment, training, understanding of flood flow and patterns; need to co-ordinate effort and put in place flood crisis management plans

5. COST

5.1 Who pays? Estimated cost clear-up, repair and compensation 2012 = £1.2 billion

- Government via local authorities plus EU grants
- role of insurance industry – new agreement with Government changing

5.2 setting up mechanisms to establish eligibility and proportion of compensation

Quote: Association of British Insurers "The Government has indicated it will not provide any temporary overdraft facility for the insurance industry's not-for-profit scheme, which makes it very difficult for it to go ahead. As a result, negotiations have hit an impasse." Insurance Journal. 26 November 2012. Retrieved 1 December 2012.

Mini-conclusion: need for measures to fund flood reaction and restitution costs; agreement with Association of British Insurers essential

6. PREVENTION

6.1 The UK as a whole – different jurisdictions (Scotland/England and Wales). Government has to:

- provide aid for clean-up as a matter of urgency
- identify methods for monitoring, controlling and prevention by establishing UK-wide laws/rules/guidelines/codes of conduct in line with UK statutes and relevant EU Directives e.g.
  - Flood Risk Management (Scotland) Act 2009
  - Flood and Water Management Act 2010
  - Flood Risk Management (Flood Protection Schemes, Potentially Vulnerable Areas and Local Plan Districts) (Scotland) Regulations 2010

Mini-conclusion: need for holistic and co-ordinated approach to ensure that any flood crisis can be dealt with as expediently as possible.

7. CONCLUSION

Implications are essentially of practical nature that rest on good preventive measures

Summary of mini conclusions

- **environment**: long-term impact diff to estimate
- **community**: long-term impact with continuing threat of repetition; loss of income or livelihood
- **crisis management**: need for specialist equipment, training, understanding of flood flow and patterns; need to co-ordinate effort and put in place flood crisis management plans
- **cost**: need for measures to fund flood reaction and restitution costs; agreement with Association of British Insurers

- **prevention**: need for holistic and co-ordinated approach to ensure that any flood crisis can be dealt with as expediently as possible

Thus

- general economic effect diverse: loss of income [at best]; loss of livelihood [at worst]
- may irrevocably damage community structure in terms of demographic movements, but also polarise community between those living in flood risk areas and those not in danger areas
- seen as preventable but still a drain on local and national resources since from the Treasury i.e. via taxation affecting country as a whole.

APPENDIX 5 INTRODUCTIONS AND CONCLUSIONS - WEAK OR STRONG?

This appendix provides examples of introductions (**Table 5.1a**) and conclusions (Table 5.1b) based on the model plan outlined in **Appendix 4**. By comparing their weaknesses and strengths, you will become more aware of the types of errors that can lead to loss of marks and approaches that can earn marks (**Ch 9** and **Appendix 3**).

Sample task: *Consider the implications of extreme flooding in the UK over the last decade.*

Table A5.1a **Comparison of weak and strong introductions.**

	Introductions	Commentary
1	Apart from flooding that occurs as a result of poor drainage systems and sudden rain downpours, the most common reason for people needing to move out of their homes is because they have leaking pipes. TV overplays the flooding as a problem and so we have an exaggerated view of it as a phenomenon. In this paper, the principal problems of urban and rural flooding will be examined.	**Very weak.** This introduction does not follow the 'general-specific' format (**Ch 8**).The first two sentences are opinions that are not supported. They bear no relation to the third sentence which states the writer's intention for the content of the essay.
2	According to a Dutch proverb, 'After high floods come low ebbs'. Thus, in the case of flooding we have the phenomenon of people suddenly losing their homes and their livelihoods. This is not their fault and they have to rely on others to help them. This paper is about that help.	**Very weak.** This is not badly written but it fails to give any real context to the discussion and only provides a very general idea of what the paper will cover. Using a proverb or quotation or a definition is not always an appropriate strategy for introducing an academic paper – use with caution.

	Introductions	Commentary
3	Historically, the incidence of major flooding events is well-documented. In the last 10 years or so, there is a perception that such events have increased in magnitude and frequency. The cost that major incidents involving flood-water incur is regarded as excessive – as much as £1.2 billion for 2012 alone. This paper aims to examine the main reasons for the flooding, how it affects individuals, the involvement of emergency services and what needs to be done to help prevent major flood alerts and subsequent flooding.	**Weak.** While this roughly follows the 'general-specific' format, the first paragraph does not provide the framework for the 'statement of intent' in the second paragraph. The stated intention needs to reflect and draw from the information about the context. A paper should not 'aim to', better to be assertive and state: this paper will examine…'.
4	In this essay, I am going to talk about the implications of extreme flooding in the UK over the last decade. First of all, I shall look at 15 examples of flooding over the last decade, then after that I will examine what caused them and after that I'll spend some time on looking at what we can do to prevent floods in future.	**Inappropriate and weak.** The way this is written is very poor. It uses a colloquial style – language of 'talking' is out of place in a piece of writing. Using the words of the task is only 'padding' the paper. The 15 examples suggests a descriptive narrative lacking focus. Too strong on detail and weak on incisive analysis.
5	Most flooding across the UK in the last decade has extensively damaged infrastructure and the environment. Causes have been attributed to global warming. The impact on communities, individuals, businesses and farming is proving to be long-term in nature. The cost of crisis management, rescue, remediation and procurement of specialist equipment has to be borne by central government while personal loss is covered by insurance companies. The European model of flood management has been proposed for adoption to provide a framework for a national flood protection strategy. This paper examines the implications for communities, for crisis management and preventive action at local and national levels.	**Strong.** This introduction does follow the 'general-specific' format (Ch 8) and provides a clear statement of intent so that the reader knows exactly how the issues will be addressed in the paper.

Table A5.1b Comparison of weak and strong conclusions.

	Conclusions	Commentary
1	There is little doubt that flooding will be a serious problem for years to come. Like other problems that affect a wide range of countries, the solution to this one cannot be found easily. Through increasing co-operation, on a world-wide, national and local scale, perhaps the situation will improve in a relatively short space of time. Needless to say, it will not be easy. There are no ready-made solutions to problems of this magnitude. It will require considerable human ingenuity and good will. I hope the efforts will not be in vain.	**Very weak.** This conclusion refers to flooding in a very broad way. The points made do not really reflect the content of the essay. These are too generic and could apply to any number of subjects – not just flooding. The language is idiomatic and relies heavily on clichés which, by definition, have become meaningless. The opinion expressed in the final sentence is pointless.
2	As I sit in my study, contemplating the silver moon outside my window, I realise that the time has come to end this paper. Water is the essence of Life, whether it be in the ebbs and flows of the tides, the breezes and gales that move the trees or the migrations of birds and people across the land, water is key to all of it. The power of water has remained closest to the essential nature of Man – vital to life and work. Excess water in the form of flood is simply part of that 'ebb and flow' and we just have to learn to live with it.	**Inappropriate and weak.** This concluding 'muse' is not helpful as a conclusion. It does not revisit the task nor the discussion as laid out in the plan. It personalises the topic in an attempt to be 'clever'. In that respect it fails miserably and would drag down any mark since there is no evidence of analytical or insightful thinking.
3	This paper has touched on the reasons why excessive flooding has occurred in the UK over the last decade. It cannot be expected to diminish dramatically in the future. It can be seen that economic considerations prevail in determining how and when remedial work can be done. It depends on how the government and insurance companies agree about levels of insurance cover that can be made available. It will mean that premiums will have to increase to meet the demands made by claimants. It has been decided that more co-operation and co-ordination are required to ensure that best possible use is made of resources in times of crisis. It will be essential for local communities to have a 'flood plan' so that rescue and remediation can begin earlier. Good ideas but they will only work up to a point as the unpredictability of flooding persists.	**Very weak.** This conclusion is weak in that it strings together a number of statements – all weakly introduced by the word 'it'. This suggests that the conclusion was written in a hurry and not critiqued for style or organisation of content. This conclusion would benefit from severe editing out of some parts and reflection on the extent to which it does justice to the discussion in the main body.

	Conclusions	Commentary
4	One can conclude that, despite the uncertainties of making predictions, the pressures on government to come up with preventive measures to combat adverse weather and flooding have increased. In the developed world, flooding is a natural disaster. So, we have to use emergency services more and involve everyone in the clear-up. As far as possible implications are concerned, a greater threat of flooding may spoil economic stability regionally. Man-made measures designed to limit flooding caused it in every case.	**Weak.** Language is used to 'pad out' the text (e.g. 'one can conclude that' could be deleted). Colloquial language is inappropriate (e.g. come up with/so). Use of personal pronouns (one/ we) are language devices that should be avoided. Points not mentioned in the plan for the paper are raised in the conclusion (e.g. last sentence: absolute and non-verified terms).
5	From the discussion in this paper, it is evident that the principal reasons for flooding continue to be varied and unpredictable. The effects of flooding on communities and the economy can be identified at a number of levels. The financial and social costs affect everyone since central government has to shoulder some of the burden alongside insurers and property owners. The introduction of centrally co-ordinated and mutually supportive preventive measures and policies must be established in an attempt to minimise risk, damage and loss. Models for flood prevention strategies drawn from international, national and local initiatives will contribute to evolving such measures and so alleviate the problems that can arise during and after major flooding incidents in the UK.	**Strong.** This conclusion pulls together the key points made in the main body of the paper as laid out in the plan.

APPENDIX 6.1 OUTLINE FOR CITING SOURCES USING HARVARD STYLE

This Appendix and its companion Appendix 6.2 illustrate the use of the Harvard style of referencing which provides author and date information in the text. It is used internationally and has the advantage of being simpler, quicker and possibly more readily adjustable than other referencing styles.

How to cite the reference in the text	How to lay out the reference list or bibliography
The cause of European integration has been further hampered by the conflict between competing interests in a range of economic activities (Roche, 2009). However, Hobart and Lyon (2012) have argued that this is a symptom of a wider disharmony which has its roots in socio-economic divisions arising from differing cultural attitudes towards the concept of the market economy. Morrison *et al.* (2011) have identified 'black market' economic activity in post-reunification Germany as one which exemplified this most markedly. Scott (2012) suggests that the black economy which existed prior to reunification operated on strong market economy principles. However, Main (2008 cited in Kay, 2010) has supported the view that black market economies are not culture dependent. Statistics presented by Johannes (2010) suggest that, in the UK, as many as 23 per cent of the population are engaged at any one time in the black economy. European-wide statistics indicate that figures for participation in the black economy may be as high as 30 per cent (Brandt, 2011).	Brandt, K-H., 2011. *Working the system* [online book]. Cardiff: Thornhill Press. Available at: http://www.hvn.ac.uk/econ/trickco.htm [Accessed 1 April 2011]. *Ferry Times*, 2012. Where the money moves. *Ferry Times*, 12 April, p. 24. Hobart, K. and Lyon, A., 2012. *Socio-economic divisions: the cultural impact.* London: Thames Press. Johannes, B., 2010. Functional economics. In M. Edouard ed., *The naked economy.* Cologne: Rhein Verlag, 2010, pp. 120–30. Kay, W., 2010. *The power of Europe.* Dover: Kentish Press. Morrison, F., Drake, C., Brunswick, M. and Mackenzie, V., 2011. *Europe of the nations.* Edinburgh: Lothian Press. Roche, P., 2009. *European economic integration.* London: Amazon Press. Saunders, C., ed., 2006. *The economics of reality.* Dublin: Shamrock Press. Scott, R., 2012. Informal integration: the case of the non-monitored economy. *Journal of European Integration Studies*, 3 (2), pp. 81–9.

Quotations in the text

The movement of money within the so-called black economy is regarded by Finance Ministers in Europe as

'a success story they could emulate' (*Ferry Times*, 12.4.11).

According to Saunders (2006, p. 82), 'black economies build businesses'.

Notes:

- There are various interpretations of the Harvard style. This one generally follows BS5605:1990.

- In this version of the Harvard style only the first word of a title is capitalised. With the exception of proper nouns, other words are in lower case. Each entry is separated by a double line space.

- If you need to cite two (or more) pieces of work published within the same year by the same author, then the convention is to refer to these texts as 2005a, 2005b and so on.

- In some interpretations of this style the first line of every entry is indented five character spaces from the left margin. However, this can create an untidy page where it is difficult to identify the author quickly.

- Titles of books and journals are italicised.

- The first date in the internet citation is the date of publication, *if available*. Thus, the 'Accessed' date as shown in the second internet reference example will always be the same or later than the published date, never earlier.

- For further detailed discussion, examples and layouts of other referencing styles, consult McMillan and Weyers, 2013a. *How to cite, reference and avoid plagiarism at university.*

APPENDIX 6.2 HOW TO LIST DIFFERENT TYPES OF SOURCE FOLLOWING HARVARD STYLE

Students can now access a whole range of material in hard copy and through a range of media. From this wide variety of source material, those who supervise particular referencing styles continue to evolve interpretations of what information and layout should be provided in reference lists. This appendix provides guidance about layout following the Harvard referencing style for some of the more common types of resource.

Table A6.2 **Reference list layout in the Harvard style for commonly used types of hard copy and online resources.**

Hard copy resources	Basic format: author surname | author initial | date | title | place of publication | publisher
Book by one author	Roche, P., 2009. *European economic integration*. London: Amazon Press.
Book by two authors	Hobart, K. and Lyon, A., 2012. *Socio-economic divisions: the cultural impact*. London: Thames Press.
Book with more than three authors	Morrison, F., Drake, C., Brunswick, M. and Mackenzie, V., 2011. *Europe of the nations*. Edinburgh: Lothian Press.
Book under editorship	Saunders, C., ed., 2006. *The economics of reality*. Dublin: Shamrock Press.
Chapter in a book	Johannes, B., 2010. *Functional economics*. In M. Edouard, ed., 2000 *The naked economy*. Cologne: Rhein Verlag, 120–30.
Secondary reference – where the original text is not available and the reference relates to a citation in a text that you have read, then refer to the latter	Kay, W., 2010. *The power of Europe*. Dover: Kentish Press.
Journal article	Scott, R., 2012. Informal integration: the case of the non-monitored economy. *Journal of European Integration Studies*, 3 (2), 81–9.
Newspaper article	*Ferry Times*, 2012. Where the money moves. *Ferry Times*, 12 April, p. 24.

Online resources	
Internet references including e-books	Brandt, K-H. 2011. *Working the system* [online book]. Cardiff: Thornhill Press. Available at: http://www.hvn.ac.uk/econ/trickco.htm [Accessed 1 April 2011].
Internet references: e-journals online only	Ross, F., 2009. Coping with European fallout. *Journal of European Amity* [online], 5(14). Available at: http://jea,org/archive00000555/ [Accessed 11 Jan. 2010].
Journal article in print and online	Hunter, M., 2008. 'Europe: a group of friends or rivals?', *Journal of European Collaboration*, Available at: http://www.jec.org/3/35/hunter [Accessed 11 Aprill 2011].
Film, video or radio programme	Euro Yeti, 2010. Television programme. Kanal Alpha, Munich, 1 May.
Website	Transnational Co-operation Association. 2010. Available at: www.tca.org [Accessed 1 April 2012].

Notes:

- For subsequent editions of a book, write the reference in the normal way, but insert the number of the edition after the title e.g. 4th ed.
- For further detailed discussion, examples and layouts of other referencing styles, consult McMillan and Weyers, 2013a. *How to cite, reference and avoid plagiarism at university.*

APPENDIX 7 SIMPLIFIED RULES OF PUNCTUATION

Correct punctuation is vital for meaning and for getting your points across effectively. Errors in punctuation can cause an impediment to the understanding of the reader and in extreme cases can give rise to ambiguity or misunderstanding. Table A7.1 in this appendix provides a reminder of the purpose of the main punctuation marks and lists examples of their use.

Table A7.1 Punctuation marks and their uses.

Punctuation	Mark	How the mark is used
Apostrophe	'	• For possession: e.g. Napoleon's armies (singular owner); Students' essays (plural owner) • For contraction: e.g. Don't cry; I'm hungry; it's late. *As its central theme, the book considered wind power* (no apostrophe required at **its**) • Note:
Brackets (parenthesis)	[...] (...)	• Square brackets [...]: for adding words within a quote • Round brackets (...): to isolate explanatory information
Capital letter	ABC	• Starts sentences, proper nouns, seasons, rivers, mountain ranges, places, Acts of Parliament, titles, organisations
Colon	:	• Divides two ideas framed as sentences but joined by a colon, where the second sentence explains the first more fully, e.g. I hate travelling by plane: the waiting time is usually long and delays are frequent. • Introduces lists. • Introduces a 'long quote'.
Comma	...,	• Separates items in a list of three or more. e.g. tea, beer, juice and wine. • Separates part of a sentence. e.g. He came home, ate and fell asleep. • Separates additional information within a sentence. e.g. Rugby, in the main, is a contact sport. • Marks adverbs and signpost words e.g. Certainly, the results have been positive.

Punctuation	Mark	How the mark is used
Dash	–	• Marks an aside/addition, e.g. Murder – regardless of reason – is a crime.
Ellipsis	...	• Marks words omitted from a quotation: e.g. 'taxes ... mean price rises'
Exclamation mark	!	• Shows shock, horror. Rarely used in academic writing, e.g. Help!
Full stop	.	• Marks the end of a sentence. This is the end. • Marks an abbreviation, e.g., etc., i.e., p.a.
Hyphen	-	• Joins a single letter to an existing word, e.g. x-ray • Separates prefixes, e.g. post-modern • Prevents repetition of certain letters, e.g. semi-independent • Joins a prefix to a proper noun, e.g. pro-British • Creates a noun from a phrasal verb, e.g. show-off • Joins numbers and fractions, e.g. Twenty-three; three-quarters • Used at end of line to split a word that is too long for that line
Italics	*Italics*	• Differentiates text to show quotations, titles of publications in citations, species, works of art, foreign words, e.g. *déjà vu*; *et al*.
Question mark	?	• Ends sentences asking a direct question, e.g. Where?
Quotation marks (inverted commas)	'...' "..."	• 'Single quotation marks' mark exact words spoken/printed in a text. • "Double quotation marks" place a quotation within a quotation (British English). • Note that in some word-processing packages it is possible to choose between slanted 'smart quotes' ("...") and 'straight quotes' ("...")
Semi-colon	;	• Separates two or more sentences of equal importance and closely related in meaning e.g. They won the battle; the other side won the war. • Separates listed items, especially when the description of each item uses several words.

APPENDIX 8 BASIC SPELLING RULES

Spelling is tricky for many students. In English, the 'rules' are difficult to define because frequently there are exceptions to them. Table A8.1 in this appendix presents some of the fundamental rules with examples of exceptions where these occur.

Table A8.1 **Fundamental spelling rules of English.**

Number	Rule	Examples with exceptions as applicable
Rule 1	**'ie' and 'ei' confusion**	
1.1	'i' comes before 'e' (except after 'c')	belief, relief, chief *but* receive, perceive, deceive, ceiling
Rule 2	**Verbs**	
2.1	where verbs end in -eed and -ede, then the -eed ending goes with suc-/ex-/pro-; -ede applies in all other cases	-eed: succeed, exceed, proceed -ede: precede, concede
2.2	where verbs end with -ise, nouns end with -ice	prac**t**ise (verb)/prac**t**ice (noun) *but* exercise: verb and noun
Rule 3	**Double letters**	
3.1	Double final consonants before using -ing, -ed or -er when the words are single syllable and end with b/d/g/m/n/p/r/t	ro**bb**ed, ri**dd**ing, ba**gg**ing, su**mm**ing, ru**nn**ing, ho**pp**er, fu**rr**ed, fi**tt**est
3.2	Double consonant when the stressed syllable is at the end of the word	occu**rr**ed, begi**nn**ing, forge**tt**able
3.3	Double 'l' when words end in an 'l' preceded by a short vowel	trave**ll**ed, leve**ll**ed
Rule 4	**Adjectives from nouns**	
4.1	Nouns ending in '-our', drop the 'u' in the adjective form	glamour/glam**or**ous; humour, hum**or**ous

Number	Rule	Examples with exceptions as applicable
Rule 5	**Plurals**	
5.1	generally add '-s'; or '-es' if after ss/x/ch/sh	boys, cats, dogs; crosses, fixes, churches, dishes
5.2	Nouns ending in -y drop -y and add -ies	ally/allies; copy/copies *but* monkeys; donkeys
5.3	Nouns ending in -o, then add -s for the plural	photos; pianos *but* tomatoes; volcanoes; heroes
5.4	Nouns ending in -f and -fe, no consistent rule.	chief/chiefs *but* half/halves
5.5	Some 'foreign' nouns follow the rules of their own language in the plural	medium/media; criterion/criteria; datum/data; phenomenon/ phenomena (shown in singular/ plural order)
5.6	Hyphenated words formation of plurals	brothers-in-law; commanders-in-chief
5.7	Some nouns are the same format for singular and for plural	sheep, fish
Rule 6	**Prefixes**	
6.1	dis- and mis- do not add extra letters	dis+agree, mis+manage, note dis+satisfaction/dissatisfaction
6.2	double 'l' becomes single 'l' in compounds	full + fill = fulfil; hope + full = hopeful
Rule 7	**Suffixes**	
7.1	-ful, -fully, -al, -ally: adjectives formed with the suffix 'ful' and 'al' have only one 'l'	careful; hopeful *but* adverbs add -ly: carefully and hopefully
7.2	When forming adverbs, add -ly	skilfully, marginally
7.3	Adjectives ending in -ic form their adverbs with -ally	basic/basically but public/publicly
7.4	Silent 'e' usually keep -e when adding the suffix	hope + full = hopeful
7.5	If suffix begins with a vowel, then drop final -e	come + ing = coming
7.6	After words ending in -ce or -ge, keep -e to keep sounds soft	noticeable, courageous

continued

Number	Rule	Examples with exceptions as applicable
7.7	For words ending in -y that are preceded by a consonant, change -y to -i before any suffix except -ing, -ist, -ish	dry/driest *but* drying, copyist, dryish
7.8	For joins within word, do not add or subtract letters at 'join'	meanness
Rule 8	**Silent letters**	
8.1	Silent b; g; k; l; p; w	debt, gnat, knot, palm, psychiatrist, wrong
Rule 9	**Latin words in English**	
9.1	ending in -ix in the singular, end in -ices in the plural	appendix, appendices; index, indices
9.2	ending in -um in the singular, end in -a in the plural	datum, data; medium, media; stratum, strata
9.3	ending -us in the singular, end in -ii in the plural	radius, radii
9.4	ending in -a in the singular, end in -ae in the plural	agenda, agendae; formula, formulae
Rule 10	**Greek words in English**	
10.1	ending in -ion in the singular, end in -ia in the plural	criterion, criteria
10.2	ending in -sis in the singular, end in -ses in the plural	analysis, analyses; hypothesis, hypotheses

Notes:

- Creating a specialist glossary can help you learn to spell the jargon and technical words of your discipline.
- When words from other languages are absorbed into English, they tend to follow the spelling rules of the original language rather than English.
- For further points about improving spelling, consult the relevant chapters in McMillan and Weyers, 2012. *The Study Skills Book 3rd edition.*

APPENDIX 9 DEFINITIONS OF GRAMMAR TERMS

Table A9.1 in this appendix provides the grammar terms often used in written feedback on students' work. Knowledge of these terms may also assist in helping to understand and follow directions given by grammar-checking software. To expand basic knowledge and understanding of English grammar, consult an appropriate grammar text (e.g. Stott and Chapman, 2001).

Table A9.1 Grammar terms explained.

Grammar term	Explanation	Example
adjective	Describes nouns or gerunds (e.g. things, actions or concepts).	A **red** book; an **innovative** project
adverb	Adds information as to how something is done.	The student read **quickly**.
articles	There are only three in English: a, an, the. There are particular rules about using these and you will find these in a grammar book.	**A** shot in the dark; **an** empty house; **the** Highway Code
clause	Part of sentence containing a verb. If the verb and the words relating to it can stand alone, then they comprise the main clause. If the words cannot stand alone, then the verb and the words that go with it form a subordinate clause.	Cats eat mice **which are vermin.** [main clause] [**subordinate clause**]
conditional	Used to explain future possible situation, note the comma after the condition.	**If I had the time**, I would go out. [**condition**] [consequence]

continued

Grammar term	Explanation	Example
conjunction	Word that joins two clauses in a sentence where the ideas are connected or equally balanced.	The book was on loan **and** the student had to reserve it.
demonstratives	There are four in English: **this, these; that, those**	**This** house supports the abolition of smoking in public.
direct object	The noun or pronoun which is affected by the verb.	Foxes kill **sheep**. Foxes eat **them**.
future tense	Explaining things that have not yet happened. There are two forms: 'will' or 'shall' and 'going to'.	I **shall** work until I am sixty-five. They **will** come early. He is **going to** work harder.
gerunds	The gerund acts as a noun and is formed with the part of the verb called the present participle: ... -ing.	**Speaking** is easier than **writing** for most people.
indirect object	The person or thing that benefits from the action of a verb.	Tutors give (to) **students** written work. They give (to) **them** essays.
infinitive	Sometimes called the simple or root form of the verb. This form is usually listed in dictionaries, but without 'to'.	e.g. **to work**
nouns	Term used to refer to things or people. There are different types: e.g. abstract (non-visible), concrete (visible) and proper nouns (names of people, places, organisations, rivers, mountain ranges).	**Abstract nouns:** thought **Concrete nouns:** chair, table **Proper nouns:** Caesar, Rome, the Post Office, the Rhine, the Andes.

Grammar term	Explanation	Example
passive voice	Used to describe things objectively, that is, placing the emphasis of the sentence on the action rather than the actor. Although some electronic grammar checkers imply that the passive is wrong, it is perfectly correct. Often used in academic writing.	**Essays are written** by students. [**action**] [actor]
past participle	This is usually formed by adding -ed to the verb stem. However, in English there are many irregular verbs. You will find lists of these verbs in some dictionaries.	Work**ed** BUT many irregular verbs e.g. **bent, done, drunk, eaten, gone, seen, thought, understood.**
phrasal verbs	These verbs have a particle or particles (see prepositions) as one of their components. These verbs are generally regarded as being less formal in tone than single word verbs.	**Set down** (deposit), **pick up** (collect), **write down** (note), **look out for** (observe).
possessives	Words indicating ownership: my, mine, your, yours, his, her, its, our, ours, their, theirs.	**My** house and **his** are worth the same. **Mine** is larger but **his** has more land.
prepositions	Words used with nouns. Sometimes these are followed by an article, sometimes not, e.g. at, by, in, for, from, of, on, over, through, under, with.	Put money **in** the bank **for** a rainy day or save it **for** summer holidays **in** the sun.
present participle	This is formed by adding -ing to the simple verb form (sometimes involving spelling adjustments). It is used to form continuous verb tenses.	The sun is **setting**. We were **watching** the yachts.

continued

Grammar term	Explanation	Example
pronouns	Words used instead of nouns: I, me, you, he, him, she, her, it, we, us, they, them. Also words such as each, everyone.	I have given **it** to **him**. **We** gave **them** information for **him**.
relative pronouns	Words that link adjective clauses to the noun about which they give more information: that, which, who, whose, whom	This is the house **that** Jack built. Jack, **who** owns it, lives there. Jack, **whose** wife sings, is a baker. Jack, to **whom** we sold the flour, used it.
sentence	The smallest grouping of words, one of which must be a <u>verb</u>, which can stand together independently and make sense.	**The people <u>elect</u> their leaders in a democracy.**
subject	The person or thing that performs the action in a sentence.	**Caesar** invaded Britain. **Caterpillars** eat leaves.
tense	In English, to show past, present and future tense shifts, the verb changes. This often involves adding a word to show this. Some verbs behave irregularly from the standard rules. Here are three basic tenses; more can be found in a grammar book or language learner's dictionary	**Simple Past** I studied / we studied you studied / you studied s/he studied / they studied **Present** I study / we study you study / you study s/he studies / they study **Future** I will study / we will study you will study / you will study s/he will study / they will study
topic introducer (TI)/ sentence (TS)	The first sentence in a paragraph introduces the key point of the text; the topic (second) sentence explains the paragraph content.	**Skiing is a popular sport. (TI) Skiers enjoy this in winter on real snow and in summer on dry slopes. (TS)**
verb	The action or 'doing' word in a sentence. It changes form to indicate shifts in time (see tense) and who is 'doing' the action (I, you, he/she/it, we, you [plural], they).	I **work**, I **am working**, I **will work**, I **worked**, I **was working**, I **have worked**, I **had worked**.

APPENDIX 10 HOW TO SOLVE COMMON ERRORS IN GRAMMAR

Grammar errors can often be made without realising where the error lies. Table A10.1 in this appendix lists some typical grammar errors that occur in student writing and provides correct models for comparison.

Table A10.1 Common grammar errors explained.

Error	Incorrect examples (✗) and correction (✓)
1. Comparing Sometimes there is confusion with when to use a word ending in -er or -est rather than using more or most. For grammar book entry, look for **Comparatives** and **Superlatives**	Comparing two things: ✗ The debit was more bigger than the credit. ✓ The debit was **greater** than the credit. Comparing three or more things: ✗ China has the most greatest population in the world. ✓ China has the **greatest** population in the world. Countable and non-countable: ✗ There were less cases of meningitis last year. ✓ There were **fewer** cases of meningitis last year. (countable) ✗ There was fewer snow last year. ✓ There was **less** snow last year. (non-countable)
2. Describing Commas are vital to meaning where a 'wh-' clause is used. For grammar book entry, look for **Relative clauses**	✗ Toys, which are dangerous, should not be given to small children. ✓ Toys which are dangerous should not be given to small children.
3. Encapsulating Using one word to represent a previous word or idea. For grammar book entry, look for **Demonstrative pronoun**	✗ ... impact of diesel use on air quality. **This** increases in rush-hour. ✓ ... impact of diesel use on air quality. **This impact** increases in rush-hour. or ✓ ... impact of diesel use on air quality. **This use** increases in rush-hour. or ✓ ... impact of diesel use on air quality. **This air quality** increases in rush-hour. (unlikely) (Be sure that the word 'this' or 'these', 'that' or 'those' represents is identifiable in the previous sentence). *continued*

Error	Incorrect examples (✗) and correction (✓)
4. Its/it's These two terms are often confused. For grammar book entry, look for **Possessives** (its) and **Apostrophes** (it's)	✗ As it's aim, the book describes the whole problem. ✓ As its aim, the book describes the whole problem. (possession) ✗ Its not a viable answer to the problem. ✓ It's not a viable answer to the problem (It is …) ✗ Its not had a good review. ✓ It's not had a good review. (It has …)
5. Joining Words such as 'because', 'but' and 'and' join two clauses, they should not be used to begin sentences. For grammar book entry, look for **Conjunctions**	✗ Because the sample was too small, the results were invalid. ✓ The results were invalid because the sample was too small. ('Because' is a conjunction and is used to join two ideas.) ✗ But the UN failed to act. And the member states did nothing. ✓ The country was attacked, **but** the UN failed to act **and** the member states did nothing. ('but' and 'and' are conjunctions that join two separate ideas)
6. Double negative Two negatives mean a positive. Sometimes using a double negative can cause confusion. For grammar book entry, look for **Double negatives**	✗ They have **not** had **no** results from their experiments. ✓ They have not had any results from their experiments. ✗ The government had **not** done **nothing** to alleviate poverty. ✓ The government had done nothing to alleviate poverty.
7. Past participles These are sometimes misused, especially when the verbs are irregular. For grammar book entry, look for **Past participles**	✗ The team had went to present their findings. ✓ The team had **gone** to present their findings. ✗ The lecturer has did this before. ✓ The lecturer has **done** this before.
8. Preposition These should not come at the end of a sentence. For grammar book entry, look for **Prepositions**	✗ These figures are the ones you will work with. ✓ These figures are the ones **with which** you will work.

Error	Incorrect examples (✗) and correction (✓)
9. Pronouns These are used to replace nouns. The singular pronouns often cause confusion because they need to agree with the verb. For grammar book entry, look for **Pronouns**	**Singular pronouns** – anybody, anyone, anything, each, either, everybody, everyone, everything, neither, nobody, no-one, nothing, somebody, someone, something take a singular verb. ✗ Each of the new measures are to be introduced separately. ✓ Each of the new measures **is** to be introduced separately. **Reflexive pronouns** ✗ Although disappointed, they only have theirselves to blame. ✓ Although disappointed, they only have **themselves** to blame.
10. Specifying Words that are used to identify specific singular and plural items must match. For grammar book entry, look for **Demonstratives**	✓ **This** kind of mistake **is** common. ✓ **These** kinds of mistakes **are** less common. But ✓ **That** result **is** acceptable. ✓ **Those** results **are** not acceptable.
11. Subject-verb agreement Often singular subjects are matched with plural verbs and vice versa. For grammar book entry, look for **Subject-verb agreement**	✗ The Principal, together with the Chancellor, were present. ✓ The Principal, together with the Chancellor, was present. ✗ It is the result of these overtures and influences that help to mould personal identity. ✓ It is the **result** of these overtures and influences that **helps** to mould personal identity.
12. There/Their/They're These simply need to be remembered. For grammar book entry, look for **Words that are often confused** or **Homophones**. Note 'they're' is a contraction of 'they are'. Contractions are not usually used in academic writing.	✗ They finished there work before noon. ✓ **They** finished **their** work before noon. ✗ We have six places at the conference. We'll go their. ✓ We have six places **at the conference**. We'll go **there**. ✗ Researchers are skilled but there not highly paid. ✓ **Researchers** are skilled but **they're** not highly paid.

Further information on English grammer can be found in McMillan and Weyers, 2012, *The Study Skills Book* 3rd edition.

GLOSSARY

Terms are defined as used in the higher education context; many will have other meanings elsewhere. A term in **colour** denotes a cross-reference within this list.

Abbreviations:

abbr. = abbreviation

gram. = grammar term

Latin = a word or phrase expressed in the Latin (usually italicised)

pl. = plural

sing. = singular

vb = verb

Abstract Summary of the content of a piece of written work that appears at the start of a report, dissertation, thesis or journal article.

Acronym (gram.) An abbreviation formed from the first letter of words to form a word in itself, e.g. radar, NATO.

Adjective (gram.) A word that describes a **noun**, e.g. a **tall** building.

Adverb (gram.) A word that modifies or qualifies an **adjective**, **verb** or other adverb, explaining how (manner), where (place), or when (time) an action takes place. Often adverbs end in -ly, e.g. she walked *slowly*.

Ambiguous Describes a sentence, phrase or word that could be interpreted in more than one way.

Analogy A comparison; a similar case from which parallels can be drawn.

Analyse To look at all sides of an issue, break a topic down into parts and explain how these components fit together.

Annotate To expand on given notes or text, e.g. to write extra notes on a printout of a PowerPoint presentation or a photocopied section of a book.

Anonymous marking For the purpose of assessment, the process whereby a student's paper is identified only by a matriculation/identity number, rather than by name, to avoid any potential bias in marking.

Appendix Additional information at the end of a piece of writing; not essential to understanding the content of the writing, but helpful in giving detail.

Application Act of putting knowledge and understanding into practice (Taxonomy of learning objectives (Bloom *et al.*, 1956).

Argue To make statements or introduce facts to establish or refute a proposition; to discuss and reason.

Aspect Particular characteristic (of a task).

Assignment Coursework, usually completed in own (i.e. non-contact) time.

Aural Relating to the ear (something heard).

Authorities Acknowledged subject experts in a discipline area.

Bias A view or description of evidence that is not balanced, promoting one conclusion or viewpoint.

Bibliography (adjective: bibliographical) A list of all the resources used in preparing for a piece of written work. The bibliography is usually placed at the end of a document. Compare with **Reference list**.

Blurb A piece of writing used as publicity, typically for a book, and appearing on the jacket or cover.

Brainstorm An intensive search for ideas, often carried out and recorded in a free-form or diagrammatic way.

Brief The specific instructions for a task.

Capital letter (gram.) Upper-case letter (e.g. H rather than h).

Chronological Arranged sequentially, in order of time.

Citation (1) The act of making reference to another source in one's own writing. (2) A passage or a quotation from another source provided word for word within a text. See **Reference list**.

Citing Quoting a reference. See **Citation**.

Clause (gram.) Part of sentence containing a **verb**. If the verb and the words relating to it can stand alone, then they comprise the **main clause**. If the words cannot stand alone, then the verb and the words that go with it to form a **subordinate clause**.

Colloquial Informal words and phrases used in everyday speech (e.g. slang), and generally inappropriate for formal and academic writing.

Comprehension Understanding (Taxonomy of learning objectives (Bloom *et al.*, 1956)).

Concept A notion or theory.

Conjecture A supposition or guess.

Consonant (gram.) All letters other than the **vowels**.

Copyright A legally enforceable restriction of the copying and publishing of original works; only author(s) assignee(s) or their agents can sell copies.

Critical thinking The examination of facts, concepts and ideas in an objective manner. The ability to evaluate opinion and information systematically, clearly and with purpose.

Curriculum Syllabus or subjects in a course of study.

Describe To state how something looks, happens or works.

Discourse marker A word or phrase that indicates a change in direction in text e.g. however, moreover, nevertheless.

Ebrary Commercial software used to distribute and access electronic documents, such as e-books and e-journals.

Ellipsis (gram.) The replacement of words deliberately omitted from the text by three dots, e.g. 'A range of online … methods of delivering materials and resources for learning'.

Evidence Support or verification of a disputed or unconfirmed fact.

Exemplify To provide an example of something.

External examiner An examiner from outside the institution whose role is to ensure that standards of examination are maintained.

Fact A truth or real state of things.

Fallacy A logically erroneous argument used in reasoning or debate.

Feedback The written comments provided by the marker, usually directly on a student's coursework or exam script, or verbal comments communicated to the student.

Finger tracing The act of running your finger immediately below the line of text being read to follow your eyes' path across a page, starting and stopping a word or two from either side.

Formative assessment An assessment or exercise with the primary aim of providing feedback on performance, not just from the grade given, but also from comments provided by the examiner. Strictly, such assessments do not count towards a module or degree grade, but marks are often allocated as an inducement to perform well. See **Summative assessment**.

Genre A particular style or category of works of art; especially a type of literary work characterised by a particular form, style or purpose.

Gist The essence of something, e.g. a summary or a list of key ideas from a piece of writing or a talk.

Glossary A list of terms and their meanings (such as this list).

Headword The main entry for a word listed in a dictionary.

Hierarchical The quality of having a set classification structure with strict guidelines of position.

Hypothesis A proposition that is presented for the sake of argument.

Ibid. **(abbr., Latin)** Short for **ibidem**, meaning 'in the same place'; especially used in some referencing systems, e.g. Chicago style of referencing, when referring to the immediately previous source mentioned.

Ideas Used in the academic context for collective notions, thoughts or impressions.

Idiom (gram.) (adjective: idiomatic) A form of language used in everyday speech and understood by native speakers, but whose meaning is not immediately apparent from the actual words used, e.g. to 'pull someone's leg' (make them believe something that is not true).

Indentation In text layout, the positioning of text (usually three to five character spaces in) from the margin to indicate a new paragraph.

Information literacy A suite of skills that are required to find, access, analyse, create, evaluate and use information in all its formats, whether in print or online.

Instruction words The words indicating what should be done; in an exam question or instruction, the verbs or associated words that define what the examiner expects of the person answering.

Intellectual property (IP) A work or invention created by an individual and to which they can claim ownership.

Inverted commas See Quotation.

Journal A collection of academic papers published at regular intervals over a year.

Knowledge Information that enlightens understanding.

Landscape position The positioning of paper so that the 'long' side is horizontal. See also **Portrait position**.

Lateral thinking A way of examining problems by thinking about them in non-traditional ways.

Learning objective What students should be able to accomplish having participated in a course or one of its elements, such as a lecture, and having carried out any other activities, such as further reading, that are specified. Often closely related to what students should be able to demonstrate under examination.

Learning outcome Similar to a learning objective, often focusing on some product that a student should be able to demonstrate, possibly under examination.

Legend The key to a diagram, chart or graph, e.g. showing which lines and symbols refer to which quantities.

Library of Congress system A library catalogue system that gives each book an alphanumeric code. Compare with **Dewey decimal system**.

Literature In the academic context, publications that explore particular topics or problems being researched.

Marking criteria A set of 'descriptors' that explain the qualities of answers falling within the differing grade bands used in assessment; used by markers to assign grades, especially where there may be more than one marker, and to allow students to see what level of answer is required to attain specific grades.

Marking scheme An indication of the marks allocated to different components of an assessment, sometimes with the rationale explained.

Mnemonic An aid to memory involving a sequence of letters or associations, e.g. 'Richard of York goes battling in vain', to remember the colours of the rainbow: red, orange, yellow, green, blue, indigo, violet.

Module An element of a course – usually assessed; length differs according to institution.

Note-making Creating notes from texts.

Note-taking Creating notes from a lecture as the lecture is delivered.

Noun (gram.) A word denoting a person, place or thing.

Objectivity (adjective: Objective) A view or approach based on a balanced consideration of the facts, that is, unbiased.

***Op. cit.* (abbr., Latin)** Short for **opus citatum**, meaning 'in the place cited'. In some forms of citation this term is used to refer to a previous citation of the same text or article.

Paragraph (gram.) A short passage of several sentences relating to the same aspect.

Paraphrase To quote ideas indirectly by expressing them in other words Compare with **Summarise**.

Parenthesis (gram.) A word, clause, or sentence inserted as an explanation, aside, or afterthought into a passage with which it has not necessarily any grammatical connection. In writing, usually parentheses (pl.) mark off text using round brackets: (hence, more generally) an afterthought, an explanatory aside.

Perfectionism The personal quality of wanting to produce the best possible product or outcome, sometimes regardless of other factors involved.

Periodical A collection of academic papers published at regular intervals over a year.

Personal pronoun (gram.) Word referring to people. Can be first person (i.e. I), second person (i.e. she/he), or third person (i.e. they); subjective, objective and possessive. Additionally, applicable to words such as 'ship', which is referred to as 'she'.

Phonetic Relating to the sounds made in speech.

Phrasal verb (gram.) An idiomatic verbal phrase consisting of a verb and adverb or a verb and preposition. See **Idiom**.

Plagiarism Copying the work of others and passing it off as one's own, without acknowledgement.

Portrait position The positioning of paper so that the 'short' side is horizontal. See also **Landscape position**.

Prefix (gram.) An addition to the beginning of a word that implies a particular meaning, e.g. in the word extract, 'ex–' is a prefix meaning 'out of', which when added to 'tract' means 'to pull out of'. Compare with **Suffix**.

Preposition (gram.) A word that marks the relation between words or phrases, often to indicate time, place or direction, e.g. at, in, to, for. It usually comes before the word it 'controls' e.g. **at** noon; **in** the bus; **to** the north.

Primary source The source in which ideas and data are first communicated.

Prioritising Ranking tasks in precedence, taking into account their urgency and importance.

Procrastination Habit of putting off to a later time what could be done in the shorter term.

Professional body An association of members sharing a professional background and that exists to further their common interests.

Pronoun (gram.) A word that may replace a noun: I, you, he, she, it, we, they. For example, 'Traffic lights are red, green and amber. **They** light in a particular sequence.'

Propaganda Skewed or biased reporting of the facts to favour a particular outcome or point of view.

Proper noun (gram.) The name of a place, person, organisation or singular feature, such as a river or mountain. Indicated in text with initial capital letters, e.g. 'The **Himalayas** are …'

Qualitative Data (information) that cannot be expressed in numbers, e.g. the colour of the lecturer's tie or the quality of life of elderly patients.

Quantitative Data (information) that can be expressed in numbers, e.g. the width of the lecturer's tie or the number of elderly patients included in a survey.

Quotation/Quoting Words directly lifted from a source, e.g. a journal article or book, usually placed between inverted commas (quotation marks), i.e. '...' or '...'.

Recto **(Latin)** The front side of a sheet of paper, in a book, the right-hand page.

Reference list/References A list of sources referred to in a piece of writing, usually provided at the end of the document. Compare with **Bibliography**.

Register (gram.) The style of language and grammar used in written or spoken form as appropriate to the context, often distinguishing formal from informal usage, for example.

Restriction The limits or bounds set on a task.

Rhetorical question A question asked as part of a talk or written work where an answer from the audience or reader is not required or expected, and indeed where the answer is usually subsequently provided by the speaker or author. Used as a device to direct the attention and thoughts of the audience or reader, e.g. 'Why is this important? I'll tell you why ...'

Rubric The directions and explanations provided at the beginning of an exam paper.

Secondary source A source that quotes, adapts, interprets, translates, develops or otherwise uses information drawn from **primary sources**.

Semester A division of the academic year (15 to 18 weeks).

Sentence (gram.) A complete grammatical structure containing at least one verb and making sense in itself.

Subject (gram.) In a sentence, the person or thing doing the action signified by the verb.

Subjectivity (adjective: Subjective) Having a view or approach based on personal opinion, not necessarily taking a balanced account of the facts.

Subordinate clause (gram.) The part of a sentence that contains a verb, but would not make sense if it were to stand alone. See **Clause**.

Suffix (gram.) An extension at the end of a word, e.g. in the word successful, '-ful' is a suffix to the word 'success'. Compare with **Prefix**.

Summarise Using own words to create a broad overview of an original piece of text. Compare with **paraphrase**.

Summative assessment An exam or course assessment exercise that counts towards the final module or degree mark. Generally, no formal feedback is provided. See **Formative assessment**.

Superscript Text, including numerals, above the line of normal text, usually in a smaller font, e.g. ^{2}. Contrast with subscript, which is text or numerals below the line, thus $_a$.

Syllable (gram.) A unit of pronunciation larger than a single sound, but generally less than a word. In English, each syllable must contain a **vowel**, or a group of vowels or consonants, e.g. the syllables in 'simultaneous' are si-mul-tan-e-ous.

Syllabus The component elements of a course of study.

Synonym (gram.) A word with the same meaning as another.

Syntax (gram.) The way words are used (in their appropriate grammatical forms), especially with respect to their connection and relationships within sentences.

Synthesis Combination of ideas and information to create a coherent whole (Taxonomy of learning objectives (Bloom *et al.*, 1956)).

Tautology (gram.) A phrase that essentially and unneccesarily repeats the same thing as another, only in different words, e.g. 'the carpet was a four-sided square'.

Taxonomy A classification.

Terminator paragraph (gram.) The paragraph that brings a piece or section of writing to an ending or conclusion.

Tense (gram.) The grammatical state of a **verb** that determines the timing of an event, i.e. in the past, present or the future.

Topic An area within a study; the focus of a title in a written assignment.

Theory A speculative expression of an idea in an attempt to explain it.

Topic paragraph The paragraph, usually the first, that indicates or points to the topic of a section or piece of writing and how it can be expected to develop.

Topic sentence The sentence, usually the first, that indicates or points to the topic of a paragraph and how it can be expected to develop.

Typo (abbr.) Short for typographical error – a typing mistake or, less commonly, a typesetting error.

Value judgement A statement that reflects the views and values of the speaker or writer rather than the objective reality of what is being assessed or considered.

Verb (gram.) The action or 'doing' word in a sentence.

Verbatim From Latin, meaning word for word, e.g. verbatim notes are word-for-word copies (transcriptions) of a lecture or text.

Vernacular Colloquial speech.

Verso (Latin) The back of a sheet of paper, in a book, the left-hand page.

Vice versa (Latin) The other way round.

VLE (virtual learning environment) Usually an in-house system that allows staff and students to access information and materials relating to a particular course.

Vowel (gram.) The letters a, e, i, o and u (note: y is sometimes classed as a vowel).

Writer's block The inability to structure thoughts; in particular, the inability to start the act of writing when this is required.

REFERENCES AND FURTHER READING

Belbin Associates, 2006. *Belbin Team Roles* [online]. Available from: http://www.belbin.com/belbin-team-roles.htm [Accessed 1 August 2013].

Bloom, B. S., Englehart, M. D., Furst, E. J., Hill, W. H. and Krathwohl, D. R., 1956. *Taxonomy of Educational Objectives: The Classification of Educational Goals. Handbook 1: Cognitive Domain*. New York: Longmans.

Chambers Dictionary, 2003. Edinburgh: Chambers Harrup Publishers Ltd.

Fleming, N., 2001–10. *VARK – a Guide to Learning Styles*. Available: http://www.vark-learn.com. [Accessed 1 August 2013].

Foley, M. and Hall, D., 2003. *Longman Advanced Learner's Grammar*. Harlow: Longman.

Information Literacy Group (2009), Information Literacy Available: http://www.informationliteracy.org.uk/ [Accessed 1 August 2013].

Jones, A. M., Reed, R. and Weyers, J. D. B., 2007. *Practical Skills in Biology*, 4th edn. London: Pearson Education.

McMillan, K. and Weyers, J., 2010. *How to Succeed in Exams and Assessments*. Harlow: Pearson.

McMillan, K. and Weyers, J., 2012. *The Study Skills Book*, 3rd edition. Harlow: Pearson.

McMillan, K. and Weyers, J., 2013a. *How to Cite, Reference and Avoid Plagiarism at University*. Harlow: Pearson.

McMillan, K. and Weyers, J., 2013b. *How to Improve Your Critical Thinking and Reflective Skills*. Harlow: Pearson.

Ritter, R. M., 2005. *New Hart's Rules: The Handbook of Style for Writers and Editors*. Oxford: Oxford University Press.

SCONUL, 2009. Society of College, National and University Libraries: The Seven Pillars of Information Literacy Model. Available: http://www.sconul.ac.uk/groups/information_literacy/sp/nodel_html [Accessed 1 August 2013].

Stott, R. and Chapman, P., 2001. *Grammar and Writing*. Harlow: Longman.

Trask, R. L., 2004. *Penguin Guide to Punctuation*. London: Penguin Books.